GUILDFORD LIFE
PAST AND PRESENT

GUILDFORD LIFE
PAST AND PRESENT

Stanley Newman

First published in Great Britain in 2008 by
The Breedon Books Publishing Company Limited
Breedon House, 3 The Parker Centre, Derby, DE21 4SZ.

This paperback edition published in Great Britain in 2013 by DB Publishing,
an imprint of JMD Media Ltd

ISBN 978-1-78091-361-2

Printed and bound in the UK by Copytech (UK) Ltd Peterborough

Contents

Dedicated to my wife June,
Belinda, Paul and Debs,
Katie and Aimee.

INTRODUCTION

Guildford is very fortunate to have a group of local historians who are genuinely interested in the town's past and recent history. They have applied themselves to producing numerous fine books on the subject of Guildford and the surrounding areas. *Guildford Life: Past and Present* aims to carry on this tradition, adding to our knowledge of events and activities that Guildford citizens have participated in and witnessed over many years. The period covered is from the 19th century through to the 21st century, but this book can only show a glimpse of how life has been lived in Guildford during this time. I hope readers, like myself, find it fascinating and enjoy learning about how the style of life in Guildford has changed over the past 150 years. I have not set out the book in chronological order, but I have tried to link subjects from page to page. There are a few pages with images of the past and present next to one another to illustrate how things have altered over the years, and the majority of pictures have not appeared in any previous publication. The photographs taken during the last 10 years are by the author, except for the GuilFest photographs. There are descriptions of royal occasions, from the coronation of King Edward VII in 1902 to more recent celebrations when Queen Elizabeth II visited the town in 2006. There are descriptions of events that involved local people, from the 1905 Beating the Bounds to 1922 Carnival Week, and more recent events such as the Passion Play, performed in the High Street, and also the Lions Club Raft Races on the River Wey in 2006. These reflect the strong sense of community in the town.

Incidents of a more serious nature include a number of fires that destroyed town centre buildings, plus a few unfortunate mishaps that occurred on the streets of Guildford. There is an account of Agatha Christie's disappearance from her abandoned car at Newlands Corner in 1926, and the small matter of a stray bullock running loose in a High Street shop. More up-to-date is a memorable day in November 2007 when Guildford welcomed home the 1st Battalion The Royal Anglian Regiment after their tour of duty in Afghanistan.

I would like to acknowledge the great assistance of staff at Guildford Institute's library in Ward Street, who have been invaluable in regards to research for this book. Grateful thanks go to Liz Markwell, the institute's administrator, for her help and understanding. Clare Miles, Guildford Institute's librarian from 1998 until 2006, warrants a special mention for her enthusiasm in the early days of my research. Volunteer at the library Richard Evans has also helped me immensely with his genial company during long hours of consulting the institute's archives.

I have had the good fortune to gain support from a number of local historians, referred to earlier, who have the same passion for Guildford and its history as me. Firstly, thanks to David Rose, who has a great insight into Guildford's past and is always eager to share his knowledge with great enthusiasm and has always offered me encouragement. The late John Sutton, who again had considerable understanding of the town's history, especially where its transport is concerned. Roger Nicolas is another author with an excellent memory for local history and also a willingness to share his recollections. Thanks also to all these supportive people, who have either loaned photographs or provided information during the compilation of this book. With grateful thanks to the following: Tom Wilkie for his brilliant aerial photographs, Gill Walker for her 1960s pictures of Guildford railway station, Dr Vanessa Lawrence CB for her expertise in the geography of Merrow Downs, Bob Green for his information on Guildford Golf Club, Hector Cooper for the loan of his Guildford City FC photographs, Bill Pollard for his help with Guildford Boy's Brigade and Michel Harper for allowing me to climb onto the roof of his nightclub to take photographs. Appreciation is extended to my daughter Belinda Newman for her gallant work in proofreading and typing out the text and her encouraging support throughout.

Genuine apologies to anyone who has contributed to the making of this book and has not been acknowledged here. I do hope you enjoy *Guildford Life: Past and Present* and that it inspires you to delve further into the town's history. There must be many more interesting stories to be discovered about life in Guildford in times gone by.

GUILDFORD HIGH STREET

Life in Guildford might have changed out of all recognition since G.S. Shepherd's drawing of this High Street scene, but we are fortunate that the town still retains a few of its fine historic buildings. Abbot's Hospital and most of the buildings in this picture are still serving the town in one way or another. One of the most significant changes to have taken place in the High Street is the loss of public houses. During the 1800s there were over 30 pubs or beer houses in this street. Today, in the area between the River Wey and the junction with London Road, there is just one that could be regarded as a pub: the Three Pigeons, *c.*1760 (in 2007 it changed its name to the Farriers). Maybe the High Street could accommodate just one more public house? Quite a few citizens of the town would be very pleased to see the Bull's Head return to the corner of Market Street.

In 2008 the High Street is once again turned over to pedestrians for part of the day. This idea started in 1972 with an experimental closure to traffic on Saturdays. It proved so popular that it was extended to the rest of the week.

Over the next few pages are photographs of six of High Street's old pubs. Most of them were also hotels, but they all had public bars that locals patronised. In 1850 the Three Pigeons was listed as an old-established and comfortable tavern. The accommodation comprised a good coffee room, several sitting rooms and comfortable bedrooms. There was also a Market Room where dinners were provided every market day (Saturday). Naturally, good stabling was also provided. All buildings to the right of the Three Pigeons were subsequently knocked down to widen the access to North Street.

More has probably been written locally about the Bull's Head than any other public house in the town. There was a great feeling of loss, even from people who had never set foot in the pub, when it closed in 1988. The building, which most likely dates from the mid-1550s, had survived as a public house from at least 1625 until its demise in the 1980s.

The Half Moon stood beside the White Lion Hotel, which is now the location of White Lion Walk. Guests' horses could be accommodated in the stables at the rear of the pub. Also, the backyard had a skittle alley and in the garden was a piggery. Residents must have used the White Lion's archway entrance to gain access to the stables and extra lodgings that were situated at the back of the building. It became necessary for the public house to be demolished in 1900 to make way for an extension to the hotel. Reputedly the town's oldest pub licence came to an end with the demise of the Half Moon.

With its imposing bay windows, the George and Dragon complemented the adjacent Guildhall's frontage very well. However, it was not the nearest pub for people who used the Guildhall. The building, sandwiched between the two properties, housed the modest Guildford Arms. Frank Apted, a staunch member of the Temperance Movement, purchased the George and Dragon in about 1867, with the sole purpose of terminating the alcohol licence of the property. This he successfully managed to do in a short space of time.

The Jolly Butcher was another pub with a long history dating back to at least the early 1700s. An application for renewing its licence in 1847 resulted in a refusal from the magistrates. The reason given was they were not too pleased that the landlord did not appear in person and that he happened to be in prison at the time. Magistrates later granted a licence in the landlord's son's name. There were numerous rooms for lodgers at the Jolly Butcher and a separate coach house with a yard and stables, which had access from Chapel Street.

Over the centuries the old building has had several structural alterations, and it was eventually rebuilt in 1890. The Jolly Butcher closed in 1927, and Hepworth and Co. Ltd, outfitters and clothiers of Leeds, purchased the freehold. Hepworth remained on the corner of Chapel Street until the 1980s.

In February 1925 the Bridge House Hotel did not appear to be a very pleasant establishment to either stay in overnight or even have a social drink in. An objection to the licence had been lodged on the grounds that it was unnecessary to the neighbourhood because there were seven other licensed houses within easy reach. It was stated by the Chief Constable that the hotel's sanitary conditions were unacceptable. A prominent architect and surveyor, who also said that the sanitation was very defective, endorsed this view. He reported that the premises only had one toilet and access to it could only be made through a passage alongside the building. Guildford Licensing Justices decided to continue the hotel's licence.

The Bridge House Hotel survived until the late 1920s, when the property had a change of use and opened as a ladies' clothes shop. Millbrook's southbound carriageway now covers the area where the passage led to the hotel's only toilet.

Here we can see the lower end of High Street in Victorian Guildford, *c.*1880, with its shops and houses close to the town bridge. The photograph was probably taken on a quiet Sunday morning – just the right time for a peaceful outing in a horse-drawn buggy. After travelling down High Street and then crossing the Town Bridge, it might then mean a sharp climb up The Mount on the ancient road to Farnham.

Now, in 2008, we cannot travel down High Street by car, let alone over the Town Bridge. Millbrook completely cuts off the approach to the River Wey, other than on foot. In 1957 a new road was proposed from Shalford Road, adjacent to the Jolly Farmer public house, to a junction with High Street opposite Friary Street, which involved the demolition of 16 houses and eight business premises. This 500-yard long Quarry Street relief road opened in February 1962. The Town Bridge stayed open to traffic until 1973, when the new Friary Bridge opened, along with the notorious gyratory road system.

HIGH STREET MARKET, 1865

These photographs are two of the earliest to be taken of a noteworthy event in Guildford High Street. They capture the last cattle market in 1865 before it transferred to its new home in North Street. With the increase in High Street traffic, it became evident that the market should move to a less busy street. The sheep are secured in their pens close to Friary Street, and the Town Bridge and St Nicolas Church can be seen in the background. Present-day traffic now cuts through the middle of the scene at Millbrook.

Looking up High Street, we can see that the pens have been removed and stacked. It seems like three men are trying to round up three young bullocks, which are not being very cooperative. Unfortunately, the cameras of the 1860s could not cope with movement, so we cannot be sure what is actually happening.

St Nicolas Church

At the bottom of High Street, across the Town Bridge, lies St Nicolas Church. We have come to assume that all our churches are of sturdy construction and have lasted for hundreds of years, and documented evidence has shown us that many have provided safe shelter for worshippers over the centuries. However, St Nicolas Church, built in 1837, was badly designed and poorly constructed from the offset. Damp was causing serious problems throughout the structure as early as 1845. A report in 1871 stated that the roof was in a dangerous state of repair, with 'rotted wall plates and decaying beams'. Dr John Monsell became rector on 11 July 1870. He also became an honorary chaplin to Queen Victoria in 1872. Monsell set about organising the building of a new church on the site. Work began on 14 September 1874, and arrangements were made for the laying of a memorial stone by the Duke of Northumberland on 2 April 1875.

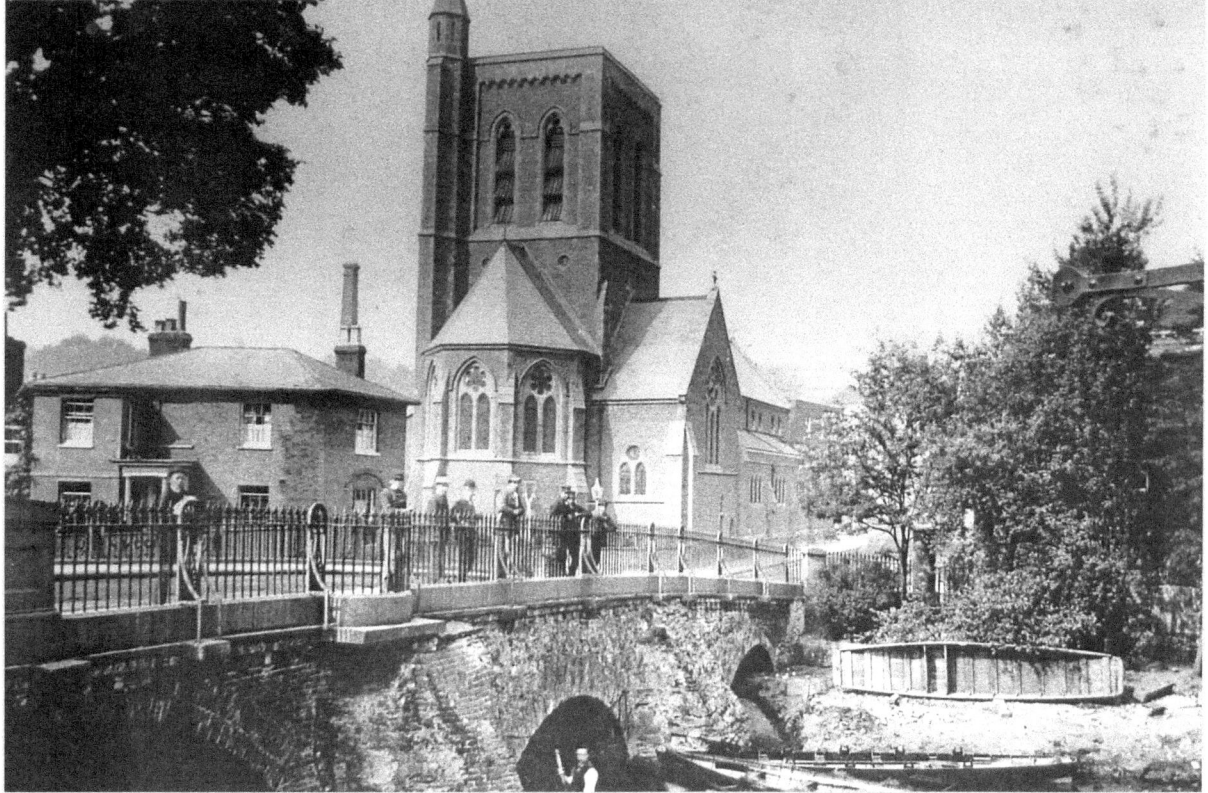

Dr Monsell's work was almost finished when, on 25 March, he fell in the churchyard, broke his arm and was unable to attend the stone laying. His condition deteriorated, and it was then discovered that he had also injured his chest. Blood poisoning was suspected. Queen Victoria sent two telegrams to enquire about his health. The man who worked so hard for his dream of a splendid new church by the river, John Monsell, died on 9 April 1875. Remains of a mediaeval pillar, which came from under the demolished tower, were erected on the spot where Monsell fell, complete with an inscription plate. It remained there for over 100 years, until the stone crumbled and it had to be removed in 1977. The photograph of the new St Nicolas Church also shows Guildford's ancient Town Bridge, which was subsequently destroyed in the floods of 1900.

Pictured left is the original section of the mediaeval pillar used for Dr John Monsell's memorial. The powers-that-be had tried to preserve the stone by dressing a piece of lead over its top, but ultimately it succumbed to the elements. In 1977 a new stone and plaque, pictured right, were placed on the spot where Monsell fell.

The unveiling of a calvary memorial outside St Nicolas Church in memory of lives lost in World War One took place on 12 April 1919. A large gathering assembled, including many servicemen, on the corner of Millmead and High Street for the dedication ceremony. It is regrettable that only the plinth remains in place today. Dr Monsell's memorial is situated near the tree in the centre of the picture.

The dedication on the plinth mentions one 19-year-old soldier by name, but the memorial is for all young men who died in World War One.

St Nicolas Church is one of Guildford's original three churches, along with St Mary's and Holy Trinity. Centuries ago, when these churches were the only ones situated in the borough, Guildford was unkindly referred to as 'a town with three churches, no steeples'. There has been a church on this site since at least the 14th century. St Nicolas Church's closeness to the River Wey has resulted in serious flooding on occasions, but it has always overcome the adversity, and it remains a beautiful church.

TOWN BRIDGE

After the disastrous floods of 15 and 16 February 1900, the old Town Bridge was completely destroyed. The extent of the damage shocked the townsfolk, and the fact that the main access route to the High Street was now blocked off meant that many local businesses began to suffer. On 16 February the stone bridge finally succumbed to the build-up of pressure, and the main arch collapsed.

The old bridge had survived floods since at least 1760, when alterations were made to the structure. At that time the central arch was enlarged, and over the years repairs were made and also the carriageway was widened.

A thought to ponder here: what if the wood from Moon's timber yard had not wedged itself under the bridge in early 1900 – would Guildford's ancient bridge still be standing today?

A temporary footbridge was constructed in March 1900, while the decision to start building a new bridge took the Guildford and Surrey Councils almost a year to make. They finally agreed to share the cost of the rebuild.

On 5 February 1902 the New Town Bridge opened for use, 102 weeks and five days after the flood had destroyed the original. Mr R.W. Fielder recorded the event with this sketch of the new bridge.

During King George V's Silver Jubilee celebrations in 1935, the Town Bridge became central to the festivities and was regarded as the gateway to Guildford. A wooden arch was constructed over the bridge, complete with elaborate portcullis.

ROYAL CELEBRATIONS

These wooden arches were popular decorations for royal celebrations in the first half of the 20th century. The one that straddled the road for King George V's coronation in 1911 stretched from the corner of St Nicolas Church to the Connaught Hotel.

The High Sheriff of Surrey, Mr Hoskin Master, reads the proclamation of George V's accession to the throne from the Town Hall balcony in 1910.

George's father Edward VII became king when Queen Victoria died in January 1901. Unfortunately, the coronation planned for 26 June 1902 had to be postponed until August due to his ill health. Guildford, as with most towns up and down the country, had already organised numerous events for June. Nearly all the proposed celebrations had to be abandoned. However, it was decided to go ahead with a dinner for 'The Old People' at the County and Borough Hall because there was nothing to offend 'the canons of good taste'. It was also felt that the children's procession and tea party could proceed as originally planned.

An invitation to dinner at the County and Borough Halls in North Street was given to the senior citizens of the borough.

Children from most of Guildford's schools assembled in North Street for a procession. They then marched with the bands, who accompanied them to the sports ground in Woodbridge Road. Their route took them up North Street into High Street, past the Guildhall, into Friary Street, then Onslow Street and on to the sports ground. Children from the Church School at Stoke walked straight to the sports ground under the orders of Bishop Ingham (who can be seen standing to the right of the High Sheriff on the Town Hall balcony on page 21). He had insisted that due to the king's illness, as a mark of respect, they should not join in the main procession with its bands and flags. It was a general view in the town, though, that the king would not have wanted to spoil the children's enjoyment.

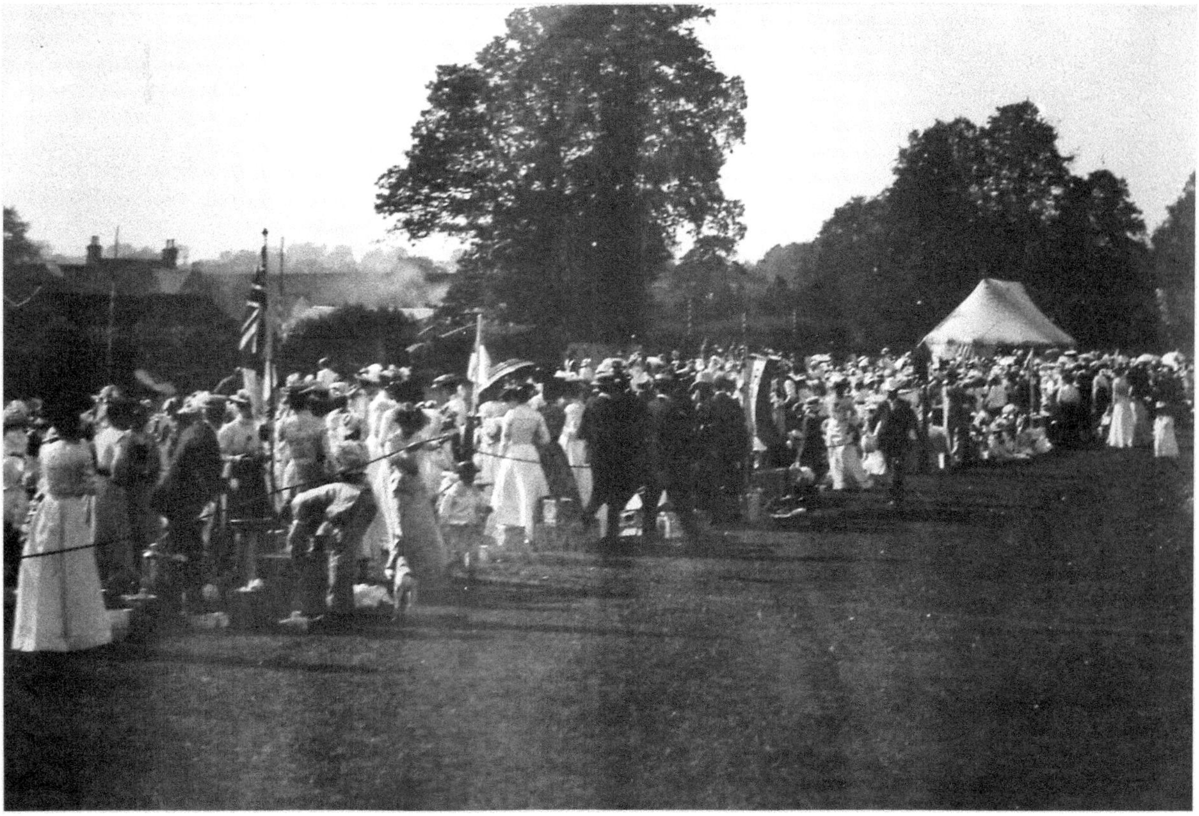

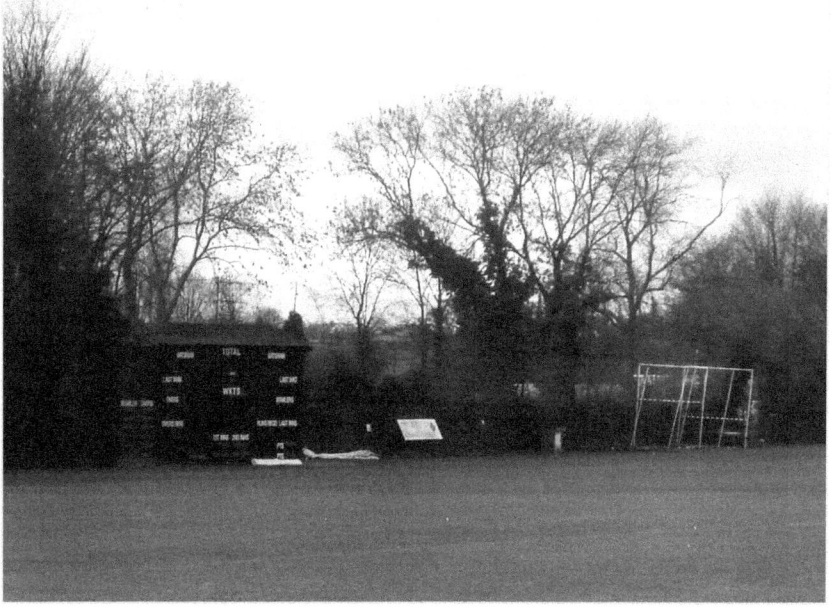

The weather stayed fine and sunny all day for the festivities. At about 6pm parents were admitted to the ground and the process of sorting out children began. They collected their offspring from what is now the scoreboard side of the ground. By 7pm all youngsters had left for home, probably tired out but with memories of a great day with their friends. What a marvellous effort the parents made in dressing up for the occasion. After all, they were just collecting their children from a party!

Nearly 4,000 children enjoyed their day of games and entertainment, arranged by their respective school. Each school had its own colour bands for identification. There were races, scrambles for sweets, and three bands played throughout the afternoon. Fireworks were released, and there were plenty of balloons. A steamroller, supplied by Mr G. Franks, provided gallons of hot water for the tea!

Official Programme.

At 2 o'clock,

The CHILDREN

OF THE SEVERAL

Elementary

Estimated to number
4,000

Schools

In the District, wearing Commemorative Medals, previously distributed to them, will assemble in North Street (south side) in order following:—

1.—Holy Trinity	Blue.
2.—S. Nicolas and Littleton	Red.
3.—Stoke	Pink.
4.—Charlotteville	Red and White.
5.—Stoughton	Blue and White.
6.—Sandfield	Red, White and Blue
7.—St. Joseph's	Primrose and White

following Bands will give Selections of Music during the assembly of the Children, viz.—

ie Band of the 3rd Batt. 'Queen's' R.W.S. Regt.
ie Guildford Temperance Brass Band.
ie Band of the Congregational School.
ie Band of the Great Central & Metropolitan Rly.
ie Drum, Fife & Bugle Band of 2nd V.B. "Queen's."

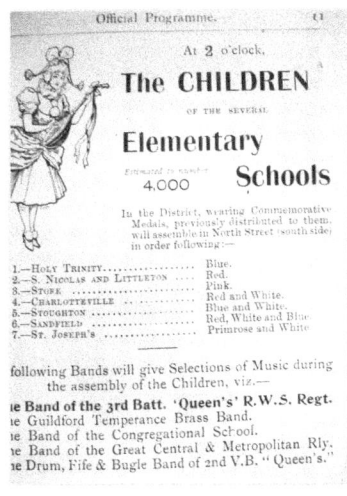

Over 100 years on, and the scenery has not changed much, apart from the scoreboard, in this 2007 photograph.

WOODBRIDGE ROAD SPORTS GROUND

The new Guildford Sports Ground was only officially opened eight years before the children's party in June 1894. The mayor and corporation attended the event, with the occasion benefiting from a sensational 'parachute' descent by Professor Baldwin, which excited the assembled gathering. Guildford is fortunate that in the late 19th century there was a public-spirited group of men who

came forward when the old cricket club ground came up for change of lease so they could utilise the area for other sports as well as cricket. A company was formed to manage the sports ground, thanks mainly to the efforts of Frank Lasham, a local businessman, who obtained a long lease from the Earl of Onslow with the option to purchase the 10-acre field.

The opening-day meeting seemed to be a multi-sport occasion. An impressive crowd stayed on to enjoy cycle races and athletic events. It appears they witnessed a very good start to the race in this particular photograph. At that time, all well-established trees lined the Woodbridge Road side of the Sports Ground. These either died or were removed many years ago. A more urban view is prevailing now.

Race meetings at Woodbridge Road became very popular at the end of the 1890s, and it was quite usual to include athletics and cycle races on the same day. The fact that both sports were included in these meetings happened to be appropriate as Frank Lasham, who worked so hard to acquire the land for the town's sports ground, was president of the athletic association and also the secretary of the cycling club.

This well-attended meeting took place on 'Whit Monday' in 1899, and it looks as though mist drifted across the ground later on in the day. It is a sobering thought to realise that over 100 years ago these local sportsmen regularly drew large crowds to Woodbridge Road, who came to support the athletic and cycling clubs and also to enjoy the competition between the town's young men.

The original cricket pavilion, with its splendid roof, seems to have been situated where the present car park stands. This gathering was for Guildford Amateur Athletics' 18th annual Whit Monday meeting in 1897. Members of the Committee and dignitaries are waiting for the last race to finish so they can award prizes to the winners.

A large embankment was built at the north end of the sports ground in preparation for the laying of a new railway line from Guildford to Waterloo via an additional station at London Road. It can be seen rising high to the rear of the sports ground, between the trees, in this photograph. This banking allowed for the track's steady climb out from the mainline station with the help of three new bridges, which crossed the River Wey, Woodbridge Road and then Stoke Road en route to London. The new line opened in 1885.

GUILDFORD'S FIRST ELECTRIC TRAIN

Guildford's first electric train travelled from Waterloo to the town not on the main Portsmouth line but on the 'new line' passing through London Road Station. On 9 July 1925 the mayor and mayoress, Mr and Mrs Rapkins, invited 300 people, including schoolchildren, to ride on the first train. From Waterloo they travelled to Dorking North, then back to Leatherhead and through to Guildford. These were the limits of the electrified line in the Guildford area at the time, although the Waterloo to Portsmouth line had been electrified through to Woking by then. Mrs Ashley, wife of Colonel Ashley – the then minister of transport – drove the first train, which carried the Bishop of Winchester among its distinguished passengers, between Dorking and Leatherhead.

Mr Albany Peters, the town crier, announced the occasion at the entrance to Guildford Station. 'Your Mayor and his brethren and divers [sundry] other persons have travelled by the first electric train on the new electric railway from Waterloo to Guildford, and I hereby declare that the line will be open to all people on Sunday next, July 12th.' The new service completed another stage of the £5.5 million electrification scheme of Southern Railway.

An official procession, led by the mayor, with members of the town council, local dignitaries and their wives, walked from the station to the Guildhall for a celebratory reception. At the luncheon, the chairman of Southern Railway, Brigadier General the hon. E. Baring, said 'No town in the world, situated 30 miles from the capital of its country, was so well served by railways as Guildford.'

One thing the 1925 electric train and any modern-day train travelling through Guildford Station have in common is that they all have to pass under Yorky's Bridge, situated about a quarter of a mile from the station itself. Thousands of university students have crossed this bridge over the years, possibly believing it was constructed for their convenience. In fact, its original beneficiaries were a flock of sheep. Long before the university or the cathedral were built, Stag Hill was farmland. When the railway reached Guildford in 1845, a level crossing was installed to allow the farmer, a Yorkshire man, to graze his sheep next to the River Wey. Unfortunately, one day tragedy struck when a train ran over a flock of his sheep on the crossing. A bridge was hurriedly built to protect the farmer's livelihood, and the bridge soon became known as Yorky's Bridge, and still is to this day.

RAILWAY TUNNEL COLLAPSE

Other dramatic incidents connected to the railways include the St Catherine's Tunnel collapse in 1895. Part of the tunnel roof and sand above fell on to the tracks and blocked the passage of an engine and its empty carriages travelling north. The driver and his fireman were not injured, but the guard received minor injuries. The only fatalities were two horses belonging to Dr Wakefield, who lived at The Beacon on top of St Catherine's Hill. Sadly, they fell into the hole that opened up after the tunnel collapsed. About 100 men worked on clearing the sand and rubble from the lines and then made the roof safe. After eight days one line was reopened for trains to travel through the tunnel again.

Photographed in about 1880, this view looks south from Guildford Station under Farnham Road Bridge towards the chalk tunnel. St Catherine's Tunnel is further down the line. Through the right-hand arch a chalk cliff face can be seen. This is the site of the present-day Farnham Road multi-storey car park.

GUILDFORD STATION

In 1887 a fan-shaped engine shed was constructed south of the bridge, after more chalk was excavated, complete with a 60-foot turntable. An extension to the sheds came in 1896, when the straight buildings, which can be seen on the left, were constructed.

On 18 September 1953 the 1512, an eight-coach train from Waterloo, failed to stop when arriving at platform one terminus at Guildford Station. As the brakes failed, the leading coach ploughed into the stationmaster's office and demolished an adjacent office. The motorman and four passengers jumped clear and escaped injury. Three men, all station staff, were trapped under the coach. All were brought out from underneath the wreckage and transferred to The Royal Surrey County Hospital in Farnham Road. Sadly, relief assistant station master Leslie Barrett died from his injuries in hospital.

Hundreds of commuters escaped injury in August 1976 when the Waterloo to Portsmouth train collided with an empty coach train as it came into platform two at Guildford Station. Miraculously, only one person was seriously injured. Mr Clapshaw, who came from Eashing, was trapped in the last carriage of the wreckage for about 30 minutes. Five other people escaped with minor cuts and bruises. The accident happened just after 6.30pm. The empty carriages from the 1734 Waterloo to Guildford train, which terminated at the station, were moving into a siding from platform four when it collided with the commuter train.

Guildford Station has a rather different look about it in this photograph compared with today. Before its demolition in 1988 it had a WH Smith & Son newsagents located on platform two instead of in the booking hall as it is now. Also, all platforms had their original Victorian pillars and roof ironwork.

This is how Guildford Station booking hall looked in 1967. It had probably changed very little from when these buildings were erected in 1884.

The late 1960s saw Arnold Ridley, who played Godfrey in the television series *Dad's Army*, at Guildford Station to publicise *The Ghost Train*, a play he was starring in at the Yvonne Arnaud Theatre.

THE TRACKLESS TRAIN

Why was this steam locomotive parked in Guildford High Street in June 1926? Over the years, there have been many theories as to why, one of those being that it was advertising *The Ghost Train*, which was playing at the Theatre Royal in North Street. Another theory was that it could have been an American film company's publicity stunt to promote a film showing at Guildford's first cinema, West's Picture Palace. The late Alf Cox, an old Guildfordian who was born in 1906, remembered it as publicity for *The Ghost Train*, but a Mr Marriott recalled that he was sure it advertised a Western film showing at West's cinema. The cinema, which opened on 8 September 1909, was located at Constitution Hall in the High Street, which later became the now much lamented Thorp's Bookshop.

There is another photograph showing the engine parked outside the Guildhall. Why did they park in front of the New Picture Playhouse first, which was on the wrong side of the road? Maybe a Western film showing at the 1920s Playhouse attracted the publicity.

Another local resident, Mr Ernest Etherton, remembered the engine being unloaded for exhibition. It was scheduled to last one or two weeks, but in fact it stayed in the High Street for several months because no one could move it! Rather than becoming a welcome distraction in the town centre, the train actually became an annoyance and was considered an unwanted eyesore by the general public. Even after it had been removed it left its legacy: rust marks on the High Street's famous granite setts remained for months afterwards.

HIGH STREET'S GRANITE SETTS

High Street's granite setts are arguably as much a part of the character and heritage of Guildford as the Guildhall Clock. Henry Peak, the first borough surveyor from 1864 to 1891, who went onto become mayor in 1899, supervised the laying of the setts in 1868 (and so the High Street setts are a lot more recent than many people might have imagined). It took over a year to complete the work at a cost of a staggering £11,000. In the 1950s it was proposed that tarmac should cover the setts to improve the surface for vehicle traffic. Fortunately, the council was against this idea. In 2008 the setts are in a sorry state of repair. They have been poorly maintained in recent years, with one of the problems being that the authorities cannot decide who is ultimately responsible for them – Guildford Council or Surrey County Council.

With the pedestrianisation of the High Street, more people walk on the road and unfortunately more people trip over the uneven setts. In 2004 Guildford Borough Council funded the laying of a flat crossing of setts near to the entrance of Tunsgate Arch. They used dressed granite in four different sizes so as to match the existing setts as near as possible. The surface is smoother now, so hopefully the accident rate has dramatically declined.

REEKS STORE FIRE, 1915

On 5 November 1915 a fire completely destroyed John Reeks & Co. Drapers Store (now the site of Tunsgate Arcade and Square) in the High Street. The fire could have spread to many of the old buildings located on the south side of the street, but fortunately it was confined to the Reeks premises and adjacent properties thanks to the efforts of Guildford Fire Brigade.

Looking from the fire scene to buildings across the street, we can just see the Bull's Head public house on the left-hand side, with the Guildhall frontage to its right.

'FEED THE GUNS WEEK', 1918

The Reeks site was cleared and the space left vacant, probably because World War One was raging and people's minds and energies were more focused on that. The eventual decision not to rebuild the store became quite fortuitous for Guildford. Just before the end of the war it was decided to reproduce a section of France's Western Front on the vacant land. It was called 'Flanders by Moonlight'. A ruined windmill depicting 'Windmill of Wassagens' stood at the back of the construction.

On 21 October 1918 'Feed the Guns Week' was opened at the site by His Grace the Duke of Sutherland with the mayor, W.S. Tavener, the corporation and the High Sheriff, Mr Renton. A large crowd of local people gathered to watch the proceedings. The idea was to secure subscriptions for war bonds and war savings certificates to a value of £250,000, and it seems that everybody subscribed to the scheme. Visitors to 'Flanders by Moonlight', local firms and individual businessmen contributed £280,197 to the fund – an incredible amount considering they were in the grip of World War One.

This section of the reconstruction was named 'The Wayside Calvary', and it depicted all that remained of the local church. A captured German howitzer cannon, seen on the right, proved a useful focal point, and this is where all the war bonds and certificates purchased by visitors were taken and placed in its breech, then a Mr G. Brierley stamped them.

Canadian soldiers of HM Overseas Forces stationed at Witley camp constructed 'The Western Front'. As the war had been raging for nearly four years, these men had most probably experienced life in the trenches of Northern France. The soldiers had even excavated beneath this site and created a crypt complete with a high altar. This replaced the one that the destroyed village church would have had. Williamson's Old English Furniture Store is the building in the background to the right. House of Fraser is located in this prime High Street position today.

THE PLAYHOUSE CINEMA

It was a fantastic effort by the Canadians in a town thousands of miles from home, but 'Flanders by Moonlight' only stood for a week, then the site returned to bricks and rubble. As a mark of appreciation, it was decided to present their general and other officers with six candlesticks turned out of Guildford oak, and photographs were given to the soldiers who had helped. This prime building site in the centre of Guildford, with its High Street frontage, was eventually cleared, ready for the construction of a new cinema.

Four years after World War One ended, Guildford Picture Playhouse and Winter Gardens Ltd opened their Playhouse Cinema, complete with an arcade and restaurant. This aerial photograph, taken in 1925, shows the large, white Playhouse building in the top right. High Street rises on the left-hand side, with Quarry Street and St Mary's Church to the bottom right.

This 1962 photograph, taken from the bottom of Pewley Hill, shows the dominant Playhouse Cinema building overshadowing Tunsgate open car park. Recently built Bridge House in Walnut Tree Close can just be seen towering over the other buildings in the centre, and the cathedral tower, which is still to be finished here, is in the top right-hand corner of the picture.

People can now stroll from Guildford's ancient High Street into the modern Tunsgate Arcade and on to Tunsgate Square, where they can enjoy a relaxing cup of tea. Little do they realise, an earlier generation visited this same spot for entirely different reasons. On the site, some experienced the reconstructed French Western Front during World War One, and then in later years cinema-goers queued to see the latest films showing at the Playhouse.

CARNIVAL WEEK 1922

During the four years of World War One, the people of Guildford lived with the fears and tragic loss of lives. Nearly 500 young men from the town died and when it ended people must have wondered whether that sense of loss and sadness would ever pass. However, in 1922, four years after the end of the hostilities, Guildfordians were ready to enjoy themselves again. A week-long carnival was organised to raise money for the Royal Surrey County Hospital in Farnham Road. The opening ceremony took place in the castle grounds on Monday 11 September 1922, although the fun had already begun the Saturday before. In reply to Mayor Rapkins's opening speech, Carnival Queen Miss Lilian Martin said 'I am greatly honoured. To cheer and brighten will be my aim. My courtiers and my friends, I come your Queen with mirth to reign, to cast dull care and gloom away. In gaiety and revelry I intend to join and ask you all to come with me. May happiness and joy irradiate our town throughout this week of Carnival. I now declare the Carnival open.'

A procession starting outside the castle grounds toured the town by way of Sydenham Road, into High Street and then through other principal streets. Floats and participating walking groups assembled at the cattle market in Woodbridge Road before moving up to the castle grounds. One of the town's old gas holders, which were removed in the late 1960s and early 1970s, can be seen in the background.

Of the many groups who joined the procession, none had more success extracting donations from the crowd lining the streets than these 12 little Charlie Chaplins. They paraded around the town pushing a pram, accompanied by an adult impersonator of the great film comedian.

The carnival queen's coach, seen here in Upper High Street, was in the form of a classic temple. Some other characters rode in another coach that had once belonged to Queen Victoria herself. It had been made in Guildford, possibly by High Street firm May and Jacobs, and could possibly be the one seen in the photograph taken at the cattle market assembly point on page 39.

Part of the procession was dedicated to an English pageant of dress between 1750 and 1850. Here the Dickens float is travelling up North Street and has just passed the old Congregational Church. The next building on the other side of Lea Pale Road was, at the time, County and Borough Halls, which held numerous events during carnival week. On Saturday evening the Push and Pull Concert Party staged a smoking concert, which attracted a full house. A sacred concert held on Sunday was also fully booked, and many people were unable to gain admission. On Monday evening a grand operatic concert was performed in the halls. So throughout the rest of carnival week, there was a varied programme of entertainment provided.

Old-style cricketers, complete with top hats, clay pipes and original-shaped bats, were also part of the procession. They did actually demonstrate an ancient game of cricket, using two stumps instead of the three that are used today.

Although there was a little rain, the procession was a fantastic success by all accounts. Thousands of spectators had turned out and packed the pavements around the route. The elegant wedding party, taking their turn to parade in front of the mayor and dignitaries on the castle grounds' bowling green, had an appreciative audience who were dressed in their Sunday best.

The bowling green must have sustained quite a pounding with all the activity that had occurred on it during the day. A cricket match had certainly been played, and a game of stoolball also seems to have been enjoyed on the green that afternoon as a stoolball board can be seen on the left of this photograph. Stoolball is a game resembling cricket, which is still played today, mostly by ladies, and apparently it is quite popular in the county of Sussex. Today's bowlers would not be too happy with all these games being played on their immaculate greens.

The carnival queen on her way to an event staged opposite Paddock Greens on the River Wey near Shalford Meadows. The mayor and mayoress and Mr Edward Cox, hon. organiser of carnival week, accompanied the queen in the motorboat.

The weather for Guildford's Rowing Club and Swimming Club joint river gala was, unfortunately, cold and dull. However, this did not deter spectators from supporting the event and lining the riverbanks. Having to cancel a few of the sports, including water polo, was a disappointment, but there were plenty of other events for the crowds to enjoy. After alighting from the motorboat, the queen was presented with a silver rose bowl by Mr Rapkins, captain of the rowing club. It was inscribed 'Presented to the queen of the Carnival 1922 by the Guildford rowing and swimming clubs.' The queen stayed to witness the fun and games of the gala, which included a ladies and gentlemen's punt-tilting contest! Apparently, the men enjoyed a race that involved the ladies putting on stockings and a nightdress then diving into the river and swimming to a winning post. Another race, one that we would not contemplate today, involved a live duck, which was released from a box at the end of a pole, and swimmers had to dive in and race to catch the poor thing. A Mr Pratt won the duck. I wonder what he did with it!

A visit by the carnival queen to Guildford's Union Infirmary, previously known as the Union Workhouse in Warren Road, led to her meeting a Mr Amey, who at the age of 89 was the oldest man in the infirmary. He was sure that he had resided in the institution long before the queen was born. She also met the oldest and youngest members of the community: Mrs George, who was 95 years old, and a baby boy, who was just 52 hours old. The men of 'the casual ward', which is better known as The Spike, cheered the queen as she left the infirmary.

The final stunt of carnival week was a pair of highwaymen on horseback who held up the traffic as it entered or left the town at High Street junction with London and Epsom Roads. They demanded a contribution to the hospital fund. Apparently, the majority of those told by the good-natured highwaymen to 'stand and deliver' entered into the spirit of the stunt and willingly handed over some cash. A grand total of £167 was collected on the day.

Above the point of the 'hold-up' there was a body hanging from a lamp-post, which, thankfully, was in fact a dummy! It had been trussed up high above the junction by the carnival organisers. Captain Hickman of the local fire brigade lent the dummy for the occasion. It was intended to be a warning to those motorists who refused to stump up any cash, but also a reminder of past times and the fate that would befall a highwayman if he was caught and convicted of his crimes. Queen Victoria's old coach became involved in one of the hold-ups – I wonder if Her Majesty would have been amused?

After a successful week of fund-raising and fun, Mr E. Cox, honorary organiser of the event, accompanied Carnival Queen Miss Lilian Martin along the upper High Street. At a meeting at the Borough Halls in October 1922, a cheque for £5,250 was presented to Sir Edward Ellis, honorary treasurer of the Royal Surrey County Hospital, by Mr Cox. Miss Martin was also presented with a gold watch, which was inscribed 'Presented to Queen of Guildford Carnival 1922'. Miss Martin declared that she would always treasure the beautiful gift. Carnival week was a wonderful week for her, and one she would never forget.

Research into the life of Lilian Martin only found a few details of her early years. She came to Guildford with her parents in 1904 and lived at 18 Eagle Road. While training to be an opera singer her health deteriorated, and she became quite ill. This curtailed her ambition of having an operatic career. When Lilian became well again, she took a secretary's position in Reading. During World War One she entertained sick and wounded soldiers with her singing in local convalescent homes. It is thought Lilian never married, and her last known whereabouts was in the 1930s when she lived in Brighton and worked as an almoner at the Royal Sussex County Hospital.

On Sunday of carnival week, an open-air church service was in held in the Great Quarry off Shalford Road. An estimated 7,000 people from all denominations attended the service. Several hundred people joined in a procession, which assembled in North Street then proceeded via High Street to Quarry Street. Crowds of onlookers watched from footpaths and out of windows, with the majority following on and participating in the service. Brett's Restaurant, now WH Smith, can be seen on the right, and it hosted a masked ball in its ballroom on the Friday. One hundred and fifty dancers attended, dressed in fancy dress costumes, creating a dazzling spectacle.

The Great Quarry turned out to be a glorious venue for the occasion. With its chalk cliffs and covering of trees around, it created a natural amphitheatre. The Bishop of Guildford, Dr Randolph, took the service and gave the address. A choir of nearly 100 voices, made up from all denomination churches within the town, led the singing.

THE GREAT QUARRY

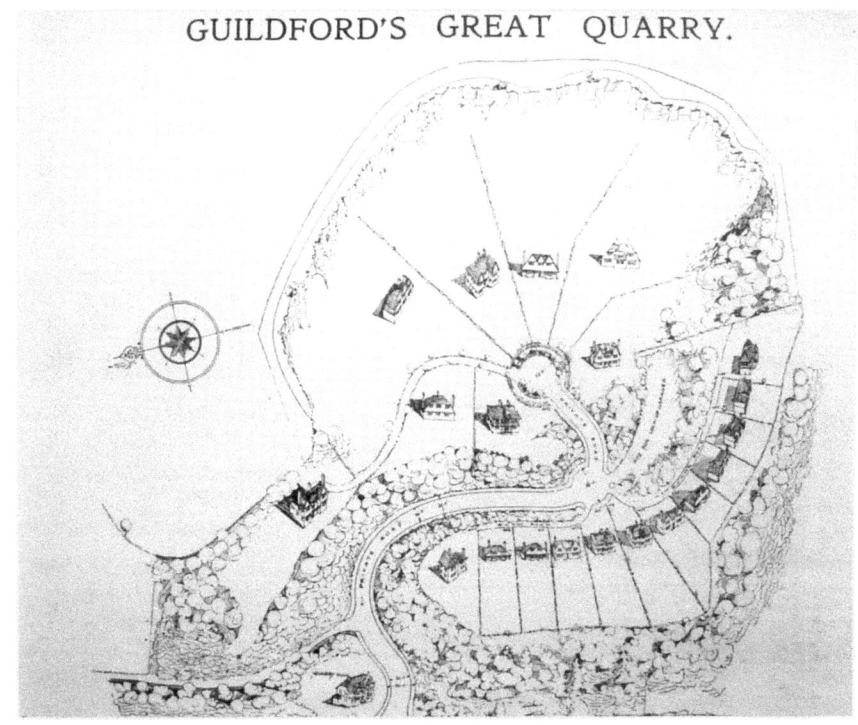

GUILDFORD'S GREAT QUARRY.

Decisions were made in the 1930s to develop Guildford's Great Quarry for residential purposes. With a prime position close to the town centre and an extensive building programme being undertaken, during that period it became an ideal location for prestige houses to be built.

It is hard to believe that in 1922 thousands of Guildford's inhabitants attended an open-air church service on this site, and for many years before that tons of chalk was excavated from the cliffs.

For many years the Great Quarry had also acted as the home of Guildford and District Rifle Club. Lord Pirbright officially opened the range on 23 July 1902, and Lady Pirbright had the privilege of firing the first shot. In 1909 the club members decided the time was right to encourage boys from the elementary schools in the borough to learn the art of rifle shooting. About 40 boys attended the initial meeting. It is most likely that these same lads became young men fighting in World War One.

Raising the Union Flag at the inaugural meeting on 3 April 1909.

The boys were taught and encouraged by older members of the club, and they showed great interest in learning the skills of handling a rifle. Here, young Guildford schoolboys are ready for their first attempt at shooting the target on an actual rifle range. It must have been an exciting experience for them.

A report of the event at the time did not mention if this was Master R. Davis's first-ever shots at a target, but the lad from Holy Trinity School, firing from over 50 yards, scored 3-2-5-4-2-4, which was quite an achievement if it was his first time.

THE RIVER WEY BY SHALFORD ROAD

As mentioned before, the chalk pit was a productive quarry, especially during the 19th century. The chalk was extracted and converted into lime. Transporting the material to waiting barges at Shalford Road Wharf involved the shortest of journeys, just across the road from the quarry, adjacent to what is now the Weyside public house. Horse-drawn barges carried the chalk along the Wey Navigation to towns and villages. Farmers needed the lime to spread over their lime-deficient fields, and they often used their own limekilns. Builders also used it for mortar and limewash.

Today, Guildford Rowing Club occupies the site where barges loaded at Shalford Wharf in the 19th century. The old quarry's chalk cliff face can just be seen through the trees behind the house on the Shalford Road.

A long-awaited footbridge was erected over the river close to Shalford Wharf in 1909. Money for this much-needed access to the river's towpath had been raised by public subscription. It was made of oak from the Weald of Sussex, and it had a clear span of 63 feet with a width of five feet. Construction took 14 weeks at a total cost of £394. Unfortunately, the bridge had to be replaced with a metal structure in 1934 because it had become too dangerous due to rotting timbers.

Mayor W.J. Patrick opened Guildford's new boathouse next to the recently constructed footbridge in May 1911. Shalford Road runs behind the fence at the back of the boathouse, and the then Jolly Farmer pub would be to the left of the photograph.

SHALFORD ROAD

Back in the 19th century Shalford Road possessed a Toll House situated on the corner with Pilgrims Way. This would have been a well-used stretch of road, with goods carried to and from wharfs on the Wey Navigation and Guildford Market. The building was removed in 1933 for road improvements to the junction with Pilgrims Way and also to widen Shalford Road.

The Shalford Road Toll gatekeeper and his family in the late 19th century, standing under the list of charges posted on the front of the Toll House. If you had arrived at the toll gate with a horse or pair of oxon drawing a cart, it would have cost you 4½d (2 pence) to carry on to Guildford with your load. A score of oxon, cows or meat cattle cost 7½d (3 pence), and a drove of hogs or pigs, calves, sheep or lambs cost 2½d (1 pence). Every two-ton weight would cost 4½d.

The Toll House, *c.*1925, looking north from Shalford Road towards Pewley Hill, with Semaphore House visible above the trees in the distance. In the 19th century Guildford Borough's boundary crossed Shalford Road, not far from this location.

Today's 21st-century view in the same direction is unrecognisable. We often despair at the loss of mature trees, but there is certainly an increase of them in this area of Guildford.

BEATING THE BOUNDS 1905

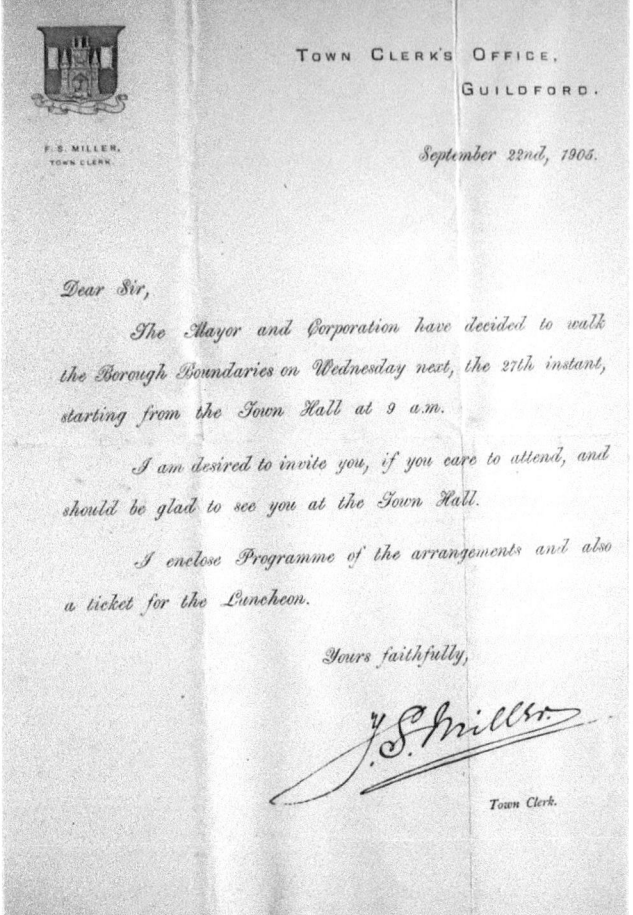

TOWN CLERK'S OFFICE,
GUILDFORD.

F.S. MILLER,
TOWN CLERK.

September 22nd, 1905.

Dear Sir,

The Mayor and Corporation have decided to walk the Borough Boundaries on Wednesday next, the 27th instant, starting from the Town Hall at 9 a.m.

I am desired to invite you, if you care to attend, and should be glad to see you at the Town Hall.

I enclose Programme of the arrangements and also a ticket for the Luncheon.

Yours faithfully,

J. S. Miller

Town Clerk.

Here is an invitation for us all to enter into the spirit of Guildford's 1905 Beating of the Bounds. This event involved a good deal of walking and some travelling in a barge on the River Wey around the new Borough boundary. Each time the town's boundary expanded, the Beating of the Bounds would take place, and this centuries-old custom also took place in 1873 and 1887. The tradition was connected to the church prior to the 16th-century Reformation. Queen Elizabeth I ordered 'That the people shall once a year at the time accustomed with the curate and substantial men of the parish, walk about the parishes as they were accustomed and at their return to church make their common prayer.' There was a great deal more to the speech, but this gives us a fair idea of the importance placed on remembering parish boundaries at that time.

The Mayor of Guildford, W.H. George, is seen here standing in the centre of the Town Hall (Guildhall) balcony, accompanied by members of the corporation, prior to setting off on their journey around the new borough boundary. Apparently, they changed out of their ceremonial robes into more suitable attire before starting their walk.

A large group of Guildford citizens had already assembled outside the Town Hall long before 9am. Prominent among them was a large group of local schoolboys who had been invited to act as beaters for the day. They must have felt a great sense of pride in being given such an important task and been eager to get started. The excitement must have been palpable. Every boy was issued with a willow stave, which was for striking the boundary stones that they would encounter on their journey. Mayor George had earlier been presented with a rod, which had a brass knob at the top, and members of the corporation were given bamboo canes. The party set off at 9.20am, led by the mayor and corporation and followed by the schoolboys and then a large crowd of local people.

They started at a slow, stately pace, proceeding down High Street and into Quarry Street, where the mayor apparently quickened the pace, and they soon arrived at Leroy's Boathouse on the Shalford Road. Once there, the main group of dignitaries boarded the 'Wey' barge, owned by Mr W. Stevens, who took the helm.

Everybody was on a mission to complete the Beating the Bounds of the extended borough boundary of 1904. After travelling only a short distance upstream to the bend in the river, all beaters alighted and started their important work, striking the first stone situated on the Shalford Road. On route to St Catherine's, a member of the party ended up in the river! As the company had just been informed that the boundary line ran along the centre of the river, maybe in his exuberance he thought he might find a stone to strike in the river.

This tradition was established with the idea that everyone who took part, being an inhabitant of Guildford, would remember the borough's range for future reference. On many occasions, in the spirit of the event, young boys were 'bumped' on the stones, so they, at least, would remember very well where the boundary lay. In this photograph, corporation members and dignitaries are seen ready to leave the barge at St Catherine's. It looks as though the schoolboys were the only ones expected to walk the complete circuit.

Beating the Bounds – St Catherine's

Leaving the barge, everybody walked back to Ferry Lane, where they turned away from the river and proceeded up the lane towards Portsmouth Road. There were over 100 boys from all over the town on the walk, including those from elementary schools – Royal Grammar School and Abbot School in North Street.

Moving up Ferry Lane, the group would have passed St Catherine's Well and maybe taken a drink from its stream. Its waters reputedly have special healing qualities. However, the beaters would not have seen the well looking remotely like this 1930s photograph, with its twee bridge. There would just be the spring water flowing from the hillside.

The beaters would probably have had a fine view of St Catherine's Chapel at some stage of their walk. This copy of a watercolour by a Miss Swaine, entitled *The Passing of the Fair*, shows the ancient St Catherine's Fair on the hill, with the chapel in the background. This was first held in 1309 and was staged annually for centuries after, except in the occasional years when it had to be cancelled for various reasons, such as the plague of 1563. In the 18th and 19th centuries the fairs often became quite unruly events. There were frequent fights between local men and fair people. It became less popular towards the end of the 1800s and finally ceased at the outbreak of World War One.

The first mention of a chapel on St Catherine's Hill dates back to 1229. In the early 1300s the rector of St Nicolas, Richard de Wauncey, decided to rebuild the ruined chapel, most likely because he received the profits as it was in his parish. The late 1700s saw the building fall into disrepair again and in danger of collapse. In 1793 Robert Austen of Shalford paid for repairs to be carried out on the chapel, so that he could still view it from his home!

The short climb up Ferry Lane was nothing compared with the terrain ahead for the hardy beaters, as can be seen in this view of St Catherine's, with the Mount and Hog's Back in the distance. Their route would take them up the left-hand side of the hill to the Old Farnham Road.

The arrival of the party on the Portsmouth Road was greeted by a large number of people who witnessed the initial 'bumping' being carried out on the stone near the gates of Braboeuf Manor. The manor entrance can be seen to the left of the horse and cart in this picture.

When the walkers reached Portsmouth Road, a lane off to their left led up to St Catherine's Hill cottages. At the time these properties were situated beyond the borough boundary. This lane could have possibly, in the view of some historians, served as the main route to Godalming many years before the railway existed. Before the present-day roadway was cut through the hill, one would have thought the poor horses pulling loaded carts or passenger coaches would have found it quite an effort to negotiate its steep sides.

Looking at the lane today, it is hard to visualise horse-drawn coaches rushing past these cottages on their way to Portsmouth, but, then again, it would seem sensible in those circumstances to travel around the hill rather than over the top of it.

Braboeuf Manor happened to be in the Parish of Artington, and this was outside of Guildford Borough in 1905. The present building dates from 1586 and is a half-timbered house with an added 19th-century stone facing. Numerous families have owned the manor, but by 1668 the Wight family were in residence. In August of that year Samuel Pepys visited his Aunt Wight and her family there. He recorded in his diary that they walked to the Red Lion in the High Street, where they dined together. Pepys's wife also joined them for the meal. Colonel Younger bought the house from the Wights in 1914 and carried out extensive restoration work on the property.

The College of Law, a registered charity, purchased Braboeuf Manor in 1964, and over the years they have made various additions to provide fine facilities for the college's students. To preserve the manor as an integral part of the college was a priority when setting up the College of Law in Guildford. Currently, there are nearly 1,000 postgraduate students on vocational legal courses at the college.

The boundary then ran across the rear of St Catherine's Coffee Tavern, located on the corner of Sandy Lane. Mayor George decided, with a few others, to walk behind the building, which was private property. The rest agreed to use the road to reach Sandy Lane. St Catherine's still has its Ship Inn 100 years on.

At the beginning of the 20th century St Catherine's possessed a second public house. The St Catharine's Inn was close to the Ship Inn on the road to Guildford. Interestingly, the name Catharine was spelt with an 'a' rather than an 'e', and the pub was also known as the Anchor and Hope. In 1847 it was described as the Anchor and Hope or Saint Catharine's Inn at Saint Catherine's Hill on the road to Godalming. In 1936 the pub was turned into a private house, and the licence was transferred to a newly constructed establishment called the Woodenbridge Hotel at Stoughton.

Returning to Beating the Bounds now, the party proceeded up Sandy Lane just a short distance before turning off into a pathway (now part of the North Downs Way) alongside Piccards Manor. The boundary line followed this path, also referred to as 'Pilgrim's Way', and went past Piccard Farm buildings. During the walk, beaters had not experienced any rain, although the previous few days they had had heavy downpours. Consequently, from Sandy Lane through to Piccards Farm, the way was very muddy in places.

They moved through fields above the farm and tracked along the hedge and fence boundary, which rose up to the Hog's Back. This part of the walk was hard work because the fields were planted with mangel-wurzels at the time. The combination of heavy soil and a steep climb caused some discomfort for many walkers.

63

The Old Farnham Road was eventually reached at 10.25am, and everybody stopped for a well-earned break. Refreshments were provided by Messrs Brett Reynard, High Street confectioners and owners of Brett's, a popular restaurant, also in the High Strett. Food and drinks were laid out on tables erected beside the roadway. This photograph shows how that same location looks today. For centuries this old track served as the main highway into Guildford from the west, entering the town via The Mount with its steep descent. Today's Farnham Road, constructed north of the old road, descends from Hog's Back with a gentler gradient.

THE MAYOR MAKES THE PACE A WARM ONE

S.T.D.

Before continuing with their journey, Mayor George was petitioned to resume at a slower pace, and accordingly he agreed to this request.

The route then passed by the War Department's Henley Fort and skirted Henley Copse. Henley Fort was one of many built in 1898 across the south east of England in anticipation of an invasion from France. Of course, this never materialised, but the fort became useful during World War Two as a Home Guard post. Surrey County Council currently use the grounds for a young people's outdoor education centre.

After striking the stone at the side of the road, it was onwards to the north side of the hill, ready for the descent into Guildford Park.

Beating the Bounds – Cornish Rebellion, 1497

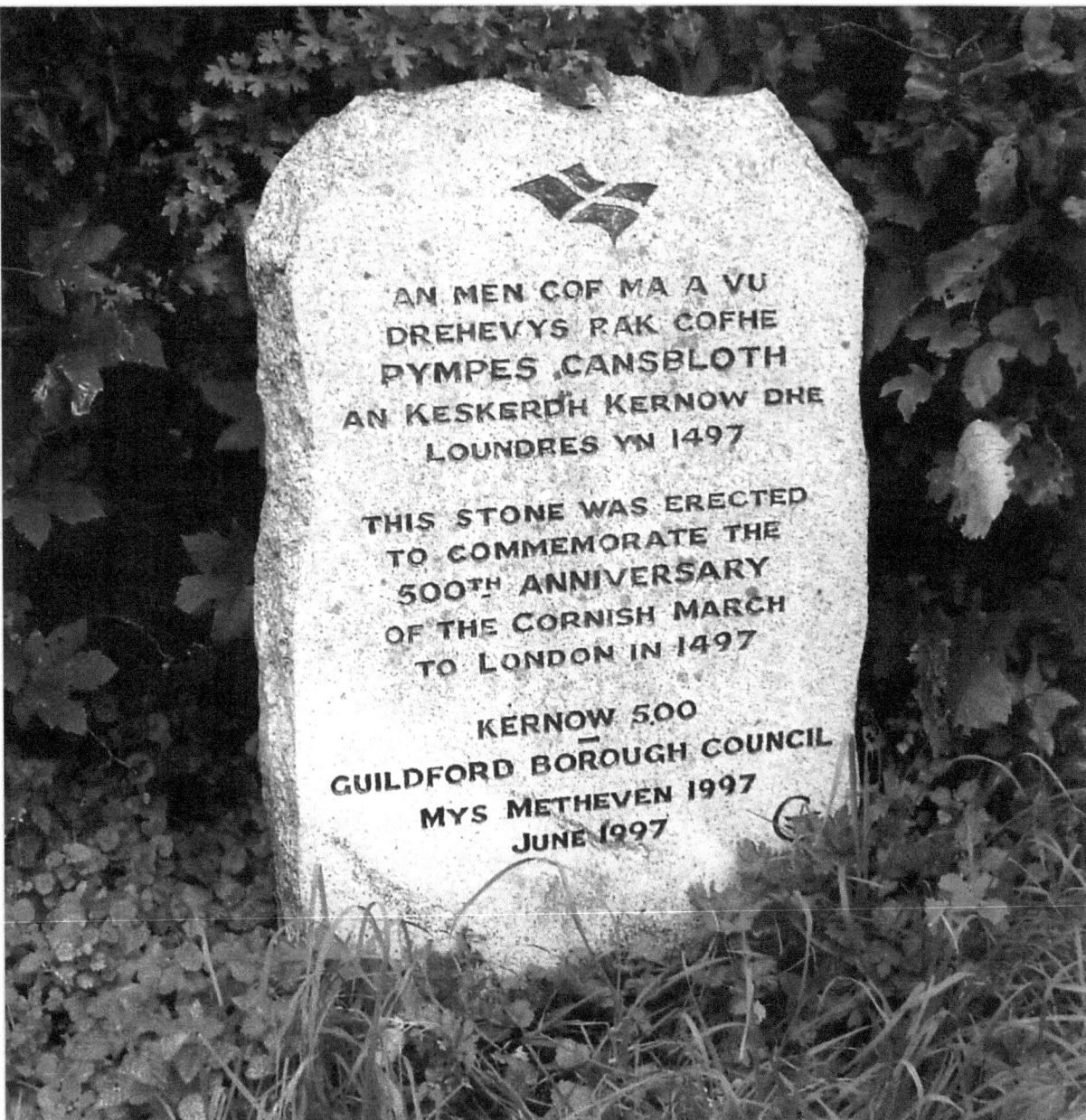

Just the other side of the gate onto the Downs, a memorial has been erected to commemorate an event that occurred here over 500 years ago. In 1497 a 15,000-strong Cornish army marched to London in revolt against King Henry VII. Michael Joseph (a Gof), a blacksmith, and Thomas Flamank, a lawyer, led the rebellion, which was in reaction to the king's tax levies to support the war with Scotland. The Cornish people had little sympathy for the English fighting the Scots, as most Cornish people were not English speakers themselves at the time. The army moved through Devon, where they received great support from the local population, then onto Bristol, across to Winchester and then Salisbury. Their march from Cornwall to the south of England made unopposed progress until they reached Guildford. The king assembled 8,000 men at Hounslow Heath on 13 June, the same day that the Cornishmen arrived in Guildford. On 14 June a force of 500 mounted spearmen rode to Guildford and clashed with the Cornish at 'Gill Down'. The Cornish army left town and moved on to Blackheath, where they pitched their final camp, looking down over the Thames and the City of London. By this time King Henry had mustered an army of 25,000 men, and the Cornish were down to about 10,000 men, due in many cases to desertion. With their inexperience, being ill-armed, badly led and without horses or artillery might, they were soon defeated and put to flight. Estimates of Cornish dead range from 200 to 2,000. Michael Joseph gave orders to surrender then fled himself, but he only reached Greenwich before being captured. Thomas Flamank was captured on the battlefield. Both were executed on 27 June 1497 and suffered the traitor's fate of being hung, drawn and quartered at Tyburn.

When the beaters arrived at this spot in 1905 they encountered farmland instead of the downland we see today. There were newly ploughed enclosures extending down to Farnham Road that had to be negotiated. Of course, the beaters would not have had this fine view of Guildford Cathedral on Stag Hill, as the building did not start work until 1937. Also, most of the houses in this recent photograph would not have been built in 1905.

This cultivated plot of neatly tended borders photographed during the early 1900s is now the playing fields for Guildford County School and the location of its staff car park.

On reaching Guildford Park the ritual of bumping continued, with a Dr Niall being dropped in the mud. The party then moved on through Guildford Park Brickworks, seen in the centre of this aerial view, which also shows the railway and Walnut Tree Close at the top of the photograph. Progress for a few fearless members of the group again became quite an effort. Mayor George and one or two others were escorted by stationmaster Mr Sumpter across the busy railway lines to Walnut Tree Close. The main group walked over Farnham Road railway bridge and linked up with the mayor on the riverbank.

Here, the lucky ones clambered aboard Mr Steven's barge once again for their journey downstream, accompanied by the strains of *God Save The King* and *Life On The Ocean Waves*. The boundary line once more ran along the middle of the river. Everyone was having such a jolly time that they failed to notice the boat had travelled some 100 yards past where the boundary turned a sharp left. This photograph shows the area where the cheerful band of men and boys alighted from their 'cruise down the river'.

On landing, the men and boys returned to the official borough boundary line and crossed over three lines of rail track leading out of Guildford Station (ladies and gentlemen, please do not try this yourselves). Negotiating the London Road line, main London to Portsmouth line and Farnham (now Reading) line turned out to be no easy task 100 years ago, in view of the great amount of rail traffic. It must have been quite a spectacle for rail travellers to see a mass of people clambering over the tracks, many with long sticks! Even more exciting obstacles had to be overcome in a lengthy journey to the rear of Stoughton Barracks.

There were steep embankments and thick, impenetrable hedges on the way. It took some time for everyone to arrive at Aldershot Road's stone, but when they did many of them were bumped, and just for the fun it – this included members of the assembled press! A cornet player sounded the National Anthem once again, and everybody moved off towards Pitch Place, up over Rydes Hill. Note how there were very few houses in this area of Stoughton in the early 1900s.

Beating the Bounds – Rydes Hill

One fine property at the time, Rydes Hill House, was adjacent to the Aldershot Road's junction with Wood Street. This Georgian house, which had some Victorian additions, became the home to Guildford brewer William Elkins in the mid-1800s. The house is now Rydes Hill Preparatory School.

The old billiard room is now the school's library, and it still has a Victorian 18-panel frieze, depicting the story of Joan of Arc around the walls.

Beating the Bounds – Stoughton

After crossing Worplesdon Road, a treacherous track on the slope of a brickyard had to be climbed. After this had been achieved, the walkers were joined by the Queen's West Surrey Regiment band, who played lively tunes on the way up towards the boundary fence of Stoughton Barracks. This photograph shows the band on their parade ground at the barracks in 1902.

In 1905 spacious fields spread from Pitch Place up through Tilehouse and Stoughton farms to an ancient lane, which extends from Grange Road to Worplesdon Road. This lane, known as Little Street, followed the line of the northern edge of the barracks. Older local residents might refer to it as 'Pig's Alley', which alludes to the time when soldiers kept pigs in this area of the camp. When the party of walkers strode out over farm fields to the sound of band music, it was over land now covered by hundreds of homes, including the recent Queen Elizabeth Park development. Before construction work could begin in 2002 on this site, the abandoned Woman's Royal Army Corp (WRACs) camp buildings had to be demolished. Originally the camp housed the training centre for the Auxiliary Territorial Services (ATS), which opened at the start of World War Two, but the barracks had remained empty since the break up of the WRAC regiment in 1992. In April of that year, the Queen Mother inspected 1,000 troops at the WRAC's last parade at Stoughton on this magnificent square.

On leaving the rear of Stoughton Barracks, walkers would shortly arrive at the pond in Grange Lane. There is a theory that this pond was the last surviving section of a moat that surrounded Stoughton Place. The 18th-century barn served the farm, which had various names for over 200 years. In the last 50 years or so, local businesses have utilised the building, which now has its address as Grange Road.

Grange Lane's ancient pond was covered over in the late 1930s/early 1940s. Many people will remember with affection the wooden structure erected at a later date on this spot. Hut Snack Bar, better known as 'Smokey Joe's', happened to be a simple café, which drew customers from far and wide to experience its individual character. The building itself started life as Northmead Boys' School's sports pavilion situated on their playing field off Grange Lane. The removal of the structure during World War Two allowed all of the field to be used for food production. For some reason though, 'Smokey Joe's' was classed out of bounds for ATS and WRAC personnel. The 1970s saw a decrease in popularity of out-of-town snack bars, and for 'Smokey Joe's' customers it was a sad day when the doors were closed for the last time.

The walkers continued on to strike a stone at Stoughton Grange. The grange, built *c.*1880 as a family home, has been divided into flats for many years.

A straight course was then taken across Reverend Paynter's Park (now Bellfield's Estate), passing Stoke Hill House on their right. Francis Paynter, who was born at Stoke Hill House in 1836, was a remarkable man. He became rector of Stoke in 1862 and remained so for 34 years. His many achievements included building three churches in Guildford: Christ Church, St Saviour's and Emmanuel in Stoughton. In 1880 Reverend Paynter purchased land on the corner of North Street and Ward Street and built the Royal Temperance Hotel. The building is now home to Guildford Institute and the Royal Bank of Scotland. He was a great supporter of the temperance movement, and he also opened many coffee bars around the town. After his death in 1908 his widow, Fanny, stayed on at the house and became a well-respected lady in the area, involving herself in the local community, especially with local children. She died in 1939, just one week short of her 100th birthday.

This wonderful 1963 aerial photograph of Bellfields shows an area where the walkers would have only encountered farmland or Revd Paynter's Park. Bellfields Court flats, seen centre left, are located on the site of Stoke Hill House. In the top right is a section of the park before construction of Bishop Reindorp School. The allotments, also top right, have long since gone, and Rowan Close has been built on the land. In the early 1960s the Woman's Royal Army Corp camp at Stoughton had major reconstruction works carried out, part of which can be seen in the bottom right. Now in the 21st century, Queen Elizabeth Park occupies all the camp's land. Before construction of the footbridge over the railway from Grange Lane to Bellfields, there was a right of way complete with a stile each side of the tracks for many years. This could well have been the route that the beaters took. In the top left corner is Slyfield Sewage Works. In 1905 this is the area where the group were heading for their sit-down meal.

Guildford Borough Council purchased Stoke Hill House and its extensive grounds in 1944 for £42,000. They bought the 184-acre estate, complete with the main house, workers' cottages and three gate lodges, from the trustees of Samuel Paynter, father of Francis, who died in 1893. The imposing mansion at the top of Stoke Hill was demolished c.1956, and now Bellfields Court's residents have that fine view from their flats. The beating party continued on their way and left Paynter's Park by way of the drive to the north gate on the Woking Road. This photograph shows the main entrance to the estate at the junction of Stoughton Road and Woking Road.

Hazel Avenue's junction with Woking Road is the approximate location of the north lodge. Crossing Woking Road, the group, looking forward to lunch, moved off at a steady pace along Woodlands Road towards Slyfield Green. On reaching The Parrot public house, their route then followed a narrow lane to the left of the pub, which led on to the sewage farm and lunch. The Parrot started out in the early 1800s as just one of the many 'beer houses' in the borough. It was rebuilt in the late 1800s or early 1900s. During this period, a number of Guildford's old drinking establishments transformed their premises from one-room beer houses to three-bar public houses. This ensured the separation by social class, with a poorly furnished 'bar' for manual workers, a 'taproom' for artisans and 'parlour' with comfortable chairs and good tables for tradesmen and clerks.

Here is the mayor and all involved in the walk taking a well-deserved rest at Slyfield. When they arrived, a welcome sight greeted them. A lunch marquee had been erected in a paddock adjoining the sewage farm, where the morning walk terminated. Not withstanding the rather unsavoury surroundings, everyone was glad of the cold food served once again by Brett Reynard. Apparently, everyone enjoyed the spread. During lunch, photographs taken by Councillor Shawcross earlier in the day were handed around. He captured the council members on the Town Hall balcony and in the boat at St Catherine's. A few speeches followed lunch, with Mayor George expressing praise for Mr Shawcross's efforts in providing photographs of the event so swiftly. Then the mayor toasted the health of the king.

The beating then resumed, and the party followed the flowing River Wey to the village of Burpham and the weir. Some difficulty was experienced in crossing here, owing to the width of the water. A fireman fell in while trying to jump, and a Mr Titley also made an attempt and met the same fate. A ladder miraculously appeared from somewhere, and this was used to bridge the gap. The services of Mr Stevens and his barge were called upon again at Burpham Weir. The Wey travelled up stream to a point where the party could disembark and follow the boundary to the London Road. Although the boat rides on the river had been rather short, all agreed that the three trips were very enjoyable. With ducking contests, continuous beating of the water and hats knocked into the river, many of which were never to be seen again, the party on the barge must have been quite a raucous sight.

From London Road, the journey took the gradual climb up Boxgrove Road, to Epsom Road, then Merrow Downs and on to One Tree Hill for tea. The next move led them to Halfpenny Lane at the crossroads with White Lane and Longdown, where Mr Newman received his 'bumping' amid great cheers from his fellow beaters. Bearing west, the bridleway followed a route across Pewley Downs to Pewley Fort. The moat here became a formidable obstacle, and, true to form, several hats were thrown in, including the mayor's!

Crowds of onlookers had assembled in this area, and Guildford Town Band played *See the Conquering Hero Comes*. Mr Shepherd at Warwick Bench kindly provided refreshments for the group of walkers. Afterwards the mayor and the chief constable escorted Mrs Parkinson to the stone, who resisted most strongly, but she did, indeed, become the first lady to be initiated into the mysterious ritual of 'bumping'. More onlookers had congregated on the Shalford Road to welcome the cheerful company back. Mayor George did not resist when carried to the last boundary stone himself and was ceremonially 'bumped', as were several others. Then the crowd sang *God Save the King*, once again!

All the Beating the Bounds sketches were by Mr S.T. Dadd of the *Daily Graphic*.

The weary walkers passed Leroy's Boathouse on the final part of their journey. It had been nine hours since the main party boarded the Wey barge that morning. This photograph, *c.*1913, was about the time that the reconstructed Jolly Farmer reopened its doors for business.

Today, the exterior of the Jolly Farmer building has not altered a great deal. The 1913 wording is still prominent on the building frontage facing the Shalford Road, although the small hanging sign informs us that the pub is now called The Weyside. Shalford Road changed dramatically in 1962 when Quarry Street's relief road was constructed. It opened to traffic in February of that year. At a cost of £53,000, it was the first major roadworks in Guildford since the bypass was built in the early 1930s.

Beating the Bounds – The Caverns

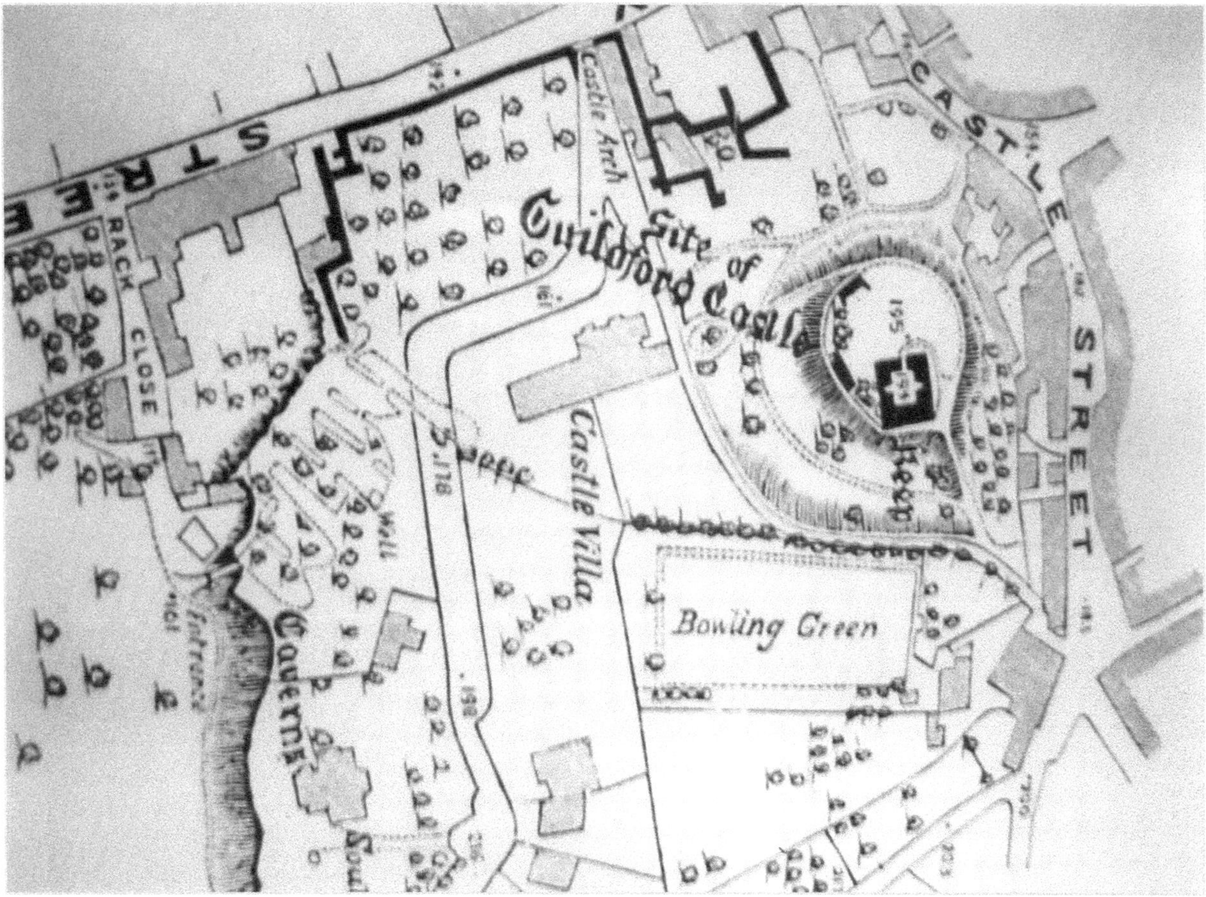

As the beaters climbed Quarry Street hill they passed by Racks Close on their right, which led up to the entrance of Guildford Caverns. These caverns were initially chalk quarries excavated, most probably, in mediaeval times for an especially hard chalk known as 'clunch'. This type of chalk is embedded in the lower walls of the Castle Keep (The Great Tower), and it was also used in St Mary's Church, as well as in Compton and Alfold churches.

The caverns consist of eight chambers, varying in width from 15 feet to 28 feet and from five feet to seven feet high. The largest extends 105 feet under what is now Castle Hill. At about the same time as the Beating the Bounds, in September 1905, Guildford Rifle Club, who used Racks Close for their rifle range, opened up the caverns and hung lanterns around the chambers. The club then gave guided tours around the passages to raise funds.

Approximately 2,500 people visited the caverns and heard the guide's various stories associated with the ancient site. At one time, the passages were thought to have connected up with the castle buildings. This idea was disproved in the late 1800s when investigations showed the nearest chamber is 100 yards from the Keep and 176 feet below ground, with 65 feet of solid chalk above the chamber roof. Legend has it that Prince Alfred, son of King Ethelbert, and 600 of his Norman followers were massacred in these caverns in the 11th century. Another event that may have some credence related to the 17th century when a report reached Guildford that the Irish had landed in England and were slaughtering everyone they came across. Panic-stricken Guildfordians – men, women and children – hid in the caverns in great numbers. Of course, the rumours of marauding Irishmen turned out to be false.

It is most likely that during the Middle Ages the caverns were utilised to store wine for the kings who resided in Guildford Castle. Over the centuries inhabitants of the town have found it difficult to find another use for the caverns. During World War One there was a proposal to store explosives, but conditions underground proved much too damp for this idea. During World War Two they were used as air raid shelters, but after the war one of the oldest and most interesting sites in the borough was declared unsafe, and the entrance was sealed. Surely we can assume some of our intrepid band of walkers taking part in the Beating the Bounds adventure would have been tempted to explore the caverns in September 1905.

In early 2008 workmen removed earth and rubble concealing the entrance to the underground chambers so that the conditions of the caverns could be ascertained for health and safety reasons. Since the 1940s it has been a very rare occurrence to catch a glimpse of the entrance or steps down from Racks Close. Only when the special chalk (clunch) is needed for repair work to Castle Arch or other parts of the castle walls is the entrance exposed. Unfortunately, it is deemed too dangerous to allow guided tours of the caverns for the general public. This is, of course, a great shame, as they would most certainly be a splendid tourist attraction for the town. While walking along passages through the various chambers, visitors might try to imagine the families, mostly women and children, who sheltered there fearing the Irish invasion over 300 years ago.

Behind the wood boarding concealing the entrance are remnants of the original doorway and passageway down into chamber one. Regrettably, this area is now covered in brick rubble.

Beating the Bounds – Quarry Street

When the walkers had reached St Mary's Church in Quarry Street, their long trek was almost over. The street they walked along in 1905 looks practically the same today, except that the mode of transport and, dare it be suggested, the children's dress sense were infinitely superior back then.

Guildford Town Band led the beaters from Shalford Road into High Street and up to the Town Hall. An immense crowd had gathered to welcome them all back to where it had begun that morning, after their 14-mile trip around the borough boundary. This may well be a photograph of the onlookers waiting to encourage the beaters on their final walk of a few yards up High Street from Star Corner. Reynard Confectioner's shop, provider of refreshments during the day, can be seen next to Angell and Son, who had occupied that building for over 50 years.

Walking up the High Street over the granite setts, the walkers must have felt a great sense of pride in their achievement of completing the challenge that day. Maybe some even had a sly glance at the lion over the entrance to the White Lion Hotel as they passed by, thinking they might make their way back down the hill later for a well-deserved drink!

The Town Hall was reached at 6.30pm, and the mayor spoke just a few words from the balcony. He thanked all those who participated in the momentous occasion and everyone who had helped organise it and make it such a special day. Finally, the walkers made their way home, no doubt tired but bursting with memories of an eventful day!

At the 7 October council meeting, Councillor Rapkins inquired as to how the expenses incurred in connection with Beating the Bounds were to be paid. Mr Rapkins mentioned that he had been asked by a number of ratepayers, who were staunch teetotallers and were fighting against the drink, who was going to pay for the whisky and beer consumed on the walk. Mayor George added, 'They had lemonade and soda water as well.' Then a Mr Lymposs added, 'And tea and coffee sir.' At that point, laughter broke out among the council members. It took another meeting before it was decided that the ratepayers were to cover the £37 expenses. Councillor Rapkins, who for some reason never wore a tie, seen here third from the right, attended Mayor W.R. Pullinger's garden party in June 1927, held at the castle grounds. Rapkins served as mayor three times in 1922, 1924 and 1925. Here he is talking to the Earl of Onslow and the first Bishop of Guildford, Dr I.H. Greig.

This is Mayor W.H. George, wearing his ceremonial robes and chains of office in 1905, his only year as mayor. Thankfully, none of his regalia ended up in the River Wey during Beating the Bounds that year!

THE GUILDHALL

There has been a hall on the Guildhall site from the 1300s onwards, and it has been referred to as the Guildhall since at least 1589. However, during the late 1800s and early 1900s it seems the building was being called the Town Hall. In 1912, though, the town council made a decision to revert back to calling it the Guildhall. Over the years, this has been where the people of Guildford congregate on important occasions. One of those times, shown here, was the proclamation of peace on 2 July 1919.

The Guildhall was decorated on 19 July 1919 for the Peace Day Celebrations, marking the end of World War One.

REMEMBRANCE DAY

On Armistice Day, 11 November 1923, the mayor and dignitaries stood on the Guildhall balcony to respect the two minutes' silence and remember the casualties from World War One. Everybody stopped what they were doing at the 11th hour of the 11th day of the 11th month – the moment the guns stopped in 1918.

In the last few years this act of remembrance has once again gathered respect, with recent conflicts now also in our minds. Here, in 2003, Mayor Gordon Bridger leads Guildford's Armistice Day two minutes' silence at 11am, which started and ended with a maroon fired from the castle grounds. A bugler sounded the Last Post from the Guildhall balcony, and people of all ages stopped what they were doing and stood still in the High Street, in shops and in offices, to remember those who have lost lives fighting for our country and for those men and women who have died in other fields of battle around the world.

Maid's Money at the Guildhall

Awarding 'Maid's Money' is a custom that has taken place in the Guildhall's council chamber since the late 17th century. It originates from a bequest made by John How of Guildford, who left £400 to be invested in government stock, and the £12 2s it produced annually was to be awarded to a live-in maid. The maid had to have worked for the same family, who resided in the old borough of Guildford, for at least two years. A contest was set up between two maids who would throw dice, and the one with the highest score received the money. John How stated that an unsuccessful competitor should be allowed to enter 'Dicing for the Maid's Money' three times, provided she still lived in the borough and remained unmarried. From the early 1900s the loser did not leave empty-handed though – they were given funds from a charity set up by John Parsons, which in fact meant that they ended up with slightly more money than the winner!

The antique fireplace in the council chambers came from Stoughton Place when the Stoughton family home was dismantled in around 1700. Stoughton Place was built as a manor house in the 16th century, probably at the time Stoughton became separate from the Manor of Stoke. Harts Gardens, off Grange Road, is most likely the site of the old house, although the Reverend Henry J. Burkitt, in his 1910 book *The Story of Stoughton,* suggested that Stoughton Grange now occupies the site.

KING GEORGE V'S SILVER JUBILEE, 1935

King George V's Silver Jubilee in 1935 saw The Guildhall floodlit for the occasion. The premises next door had the unusual name of Kitchen Late Kettle. Apparently Mr Kitchen owned the shop at that time, and the previous tenant was a Mr Kettle. In the late 1800s the property went by the name of the Guildford Arms, and in 1904 it was known to have a wines and spirits licence, and presumably it sold beer as well.

A wooden mock castle gateway was erected at the town bridge, and this greenery arch was constructed outside Abbot's Hospital. They were similar to arches created for King George V's coronation, as shown on page 21.

The town staged a grand procession in 1935, which attracted crowds of people all along the route. Fire engines are seen here in Stoke Road passing the Stoke Hotel, which for a few years went by the name Finnigan's Wake but has now sensibly reverted back to its original.

Here is another 1935 carnival float, featuring the swimming club's efforts, passing Pollard Bros Plumber's yard, an old established Guildford firm that operates from these premises today. Watching the carnival from the top of the gate to the yard are William and Eva Pollard, and Gilbert Pollard with his wife Edith. Both men, with their brother Jack, ran the business well into the 1960s.

Many families assembled on the slope of Stoke Park to view the carnival procession as it travelled along a section of the new Guildford Bypass, which had only opened that year. The carriageway cut across Stoke Park, isolating the north side from the rest of the park. The Parkway Inn now occupies the area to the top left of the photograph, and the River Wey can be seen in the background.

Taking a photograph from the same position as above causes a few problems! Brambles and sapling trees often impair the fine view of years gone by. The river is also obscured by the trees on the far side of the bypass, but it is just possible to make out the top of Stoke Mill, now home to the *Surrey Advertiser* newspaper.

THE BYPASS

It is interesting to remember that when Surrey County Council decided, in 1935, to construct a bypass for Guildford, the new road left a high proportion of the population living to the north of the new carriageway. With the town centre situated on the south side, traffic hold-ups just moved location. One problem involved traffic competing with local drivers at numerous sets of lights. Weekends became especially difficult at the junction at the Wooden Bridge Hotel, with long tailbacks past Stag Hill. In the summers of the 1940s and 1950s there would be hundreds of coaches returning from day trips to the seaside, particularly on Saturday and Sunday evenings. Children would climb aboard the stationary coaches in gridlocked traffic and ask for sweets.

Then it would be back to sitting on the Wooden Bridge's wall to check who had collected the most! This photograph shows the A3–A31 junction, with vehicles turning right for the Hog's Back, which is not possible today. Work on the Ministry of Transport scheme to widen the bypass from this junction to the Wooden Bridge started in 1958.

Fifty years later, the interchange is now only for northbound traffic joining the A3 from the A31. Again, it is noticeable that there is a proliferation of mature trees now lining the roadway, screening the view over to Park Barn. The chimney at the Royal Surrey County Hospital can be seen here left of the centre, just beyond the tree line.

STOKE PARK

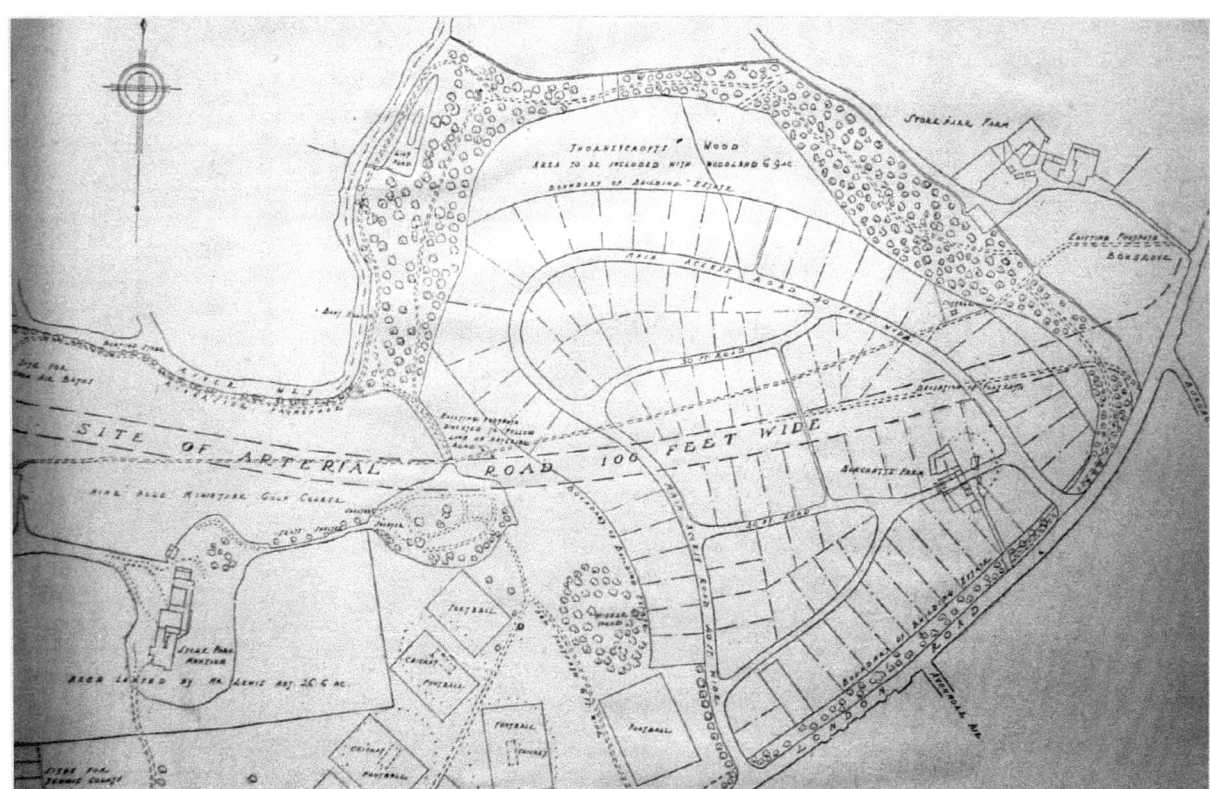

As previously mentioned, when the 1935 bypass cut through Stoke Park it isolated the northern section from the remainder of the park's open space. For 58 years this area was hardly used by the general public. Allotment holders made use of part of the land, and also the occasional travelling fair or circus was set up here. For a good number of years it served as the site for the town's Bonfire Night and fireworks celebrations. In 1929 great ideas were put forward for a new use for this area of Stoke Park. Plans were drawn up for houses to be built here, with the designs being similar to those in the adjacent Abbotswood Road. Houses along the London Road frontage were also proposed. The council purchased the parkland for £44,873 in 1925, and an idea of selling part of the land would, it was suggested, reduce the financial burden of Guildford's ratepayers. In the end, the council decided that Stoke Park should be kept solely for sports and leisure purposes, to be enjoyed by all members of the community.

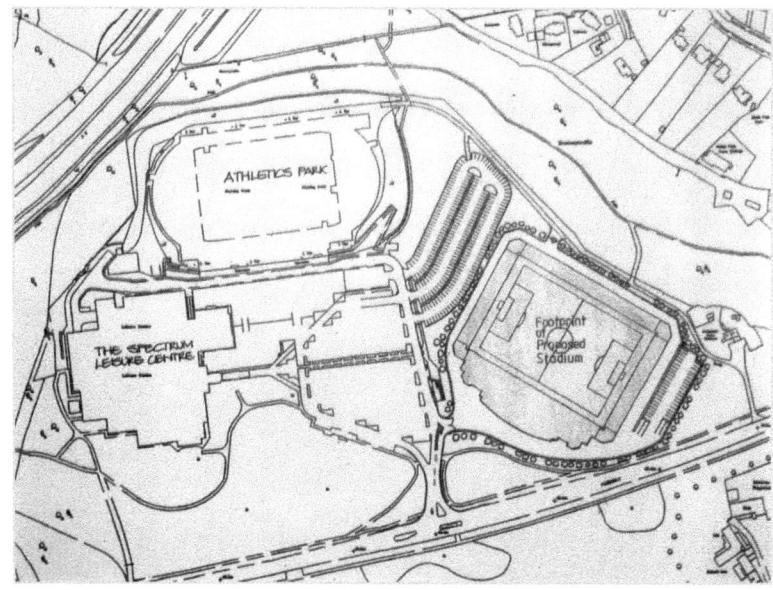

In 2008 the Spectrum Leisure Centre, with its outside athletics arena and two large car parks, now takes up most of the north section of Stoke Park. The car parks are often used for a Park and Ride scheme into the town centre, and Guildford City Football Club has shared use of the athletics arena. In 2004 local-born businessman Mr Michel Harper applied to the Borough Council to purchase the remaining piece of land. His ambition was to build a sports stadium that could be used by Guildford City Football Club and also as an events arena for concerts and arts entertainment, in keeping with the 1925 council's remit for the people of Guildford. However, the council of 2004 turned the application down.

Stoke Park – Princess Mary and the Girl Guides Rally

Since its purchase, Stoke Park has become the heart and soul of Guildford. So many activities and events have taken place here over the past 80 years or so. One such grand occasion was in June 1925 when 6,000 Surrey Girl Guides assembled in the park to parade in front of Princess Mary, Viscountess Laselles. The princess was King George V's only daughter and the aunt of our present queen.

Arriving at Nightingale Road entrance to the park, Princess Mary was greeted by a guard of honour comprising a specially selected group of girl guides from all over Surrey, who had been chosen because they had excelled in their own individual guide company. The girl guide at the end of the line certainly has many badges pinned to her arm!

The parade took place in the grounds of Stoke Park Preparatory School, which in later years became an annexe of Guildford Technical College. Unfortunately, the town lost a fine building when it was demolished in 1977. In 1925 the school grounds were the proposed site for Guildford's first cathedral, but the school governors objected most strongly. As it turned out, Guildford Council came to the conclusion that there was insufficient land that could be spared in Stoke Park to build such a large building. The consensus of opinion remained that most of the park should be left to open space for leisure pursuits.

Stoke Park – Race For Life

Stoke Park's space was fully utilised in 2002 when over 3,000 women turned out to support Surrey's Race For Life event. Organisers had to delay the start because they had only expected around 1,000 runners and walkers to take part on the 5km course. Race For Life events are organised across the country to raise funds for Cancer Research UK.

Before the race, there was a communal warm up for the 3,000 ladies. Many runners and walkers wore names of family and friends who had been affected by cancer in some way. It was an emotional day for many people remembering loved ones.

Participants of all ages circled the whole park; some sprinted, but most jogged or walked. One lady, aged 81, was believed to be the oldest woman to complete the course.

Stoke Park – Model Engineering Society

After including Guildford Model Engineering Society in *Guildford The Changing Face* in 2002, I have no hesitation in recording an event they staged in 2003. In a commanding position at the north-east corner of Stoke Park, GMES are in a good area to stage their regular open days, and there is something for everybody. This 1923 steamroller was a special attraction they displayed at an open day. Guildford Corporation purchased this very steamroller from Aveling and Porter of Rochester for £797.

The roller served the council for 35 years until 1959 when it was sold to a London scrap dealer. Mr Roger West purchased the rusting wreck from the dealer for £90 and set about restoring the skeleton structure of the machine into a beautiful steamroller, which returned home to Guildford after 44 years. Mr West used a low-loader to transport his precious cargo from Leicestershire to Guildford so society members and visitors could view and admire it.

At an open day in 2006, a fine selection of model steam engines were proudly displayed by their owners. There were some 50 or so models lined up at one time.

A must for all the family is a ride on one of the model trains that travel on the narrow gauge railway track around the one-and-a-half acre site. Guildford Borough Council provided the area of Stoke Park for GMES in 1958, and the club laid their first section of track in 1959.

GuilFest at Stoke Park

By 2006 GuilFest had held its three-day event at Stoke Park for 15 years. Top artists from around the world have performed over this time, and the music festival has become one of the most popular in the country.

Organiser Tony Scott has worked tirelessly to maintain and improve the entertainment value each year. GuilFest gained an award for the best family-friendly UK festival in 2006, with family entertainment being a priority at the festival over recent years.

Here, Suggs and Madness entertain their fans on the main stage at the 2007 festival. In keeping with the family atmosphere, their families joined them on stage for their encore! They also appeared at GuilFest in 2003, when an estimated 15,000 people sang along to hits like *Our House* and *One Step Beyond*. Later the band dedicated *It Must Be Love* to Barry White, who had died the day before.

Top acts performing at GuilFest have included Simple Minds, Paul Weller, UB40, Blondie, Lulu and Rolf Harris, but the festival also provides a platform for less well-known bands, and many local bands have taken to the stages. Here's local boy David Rose, who takes on the persona of Sammy Rat fronting Sammy Rat's Big Big Blues Band. How many people who listen to his music realise that he is a well-known local historian and writer?

PANCAKE RACES IN HIGH STREET

Here in 2006, away from running GuilFest, is Tony Scott whipping up some pancakes with Guildford's MP Anne Milton outside the Guildhall. The reason for their culinary endeavours was Charlotteville Jubilee Trust's Shrove Tuesday pancake races, which were held in the High Street. The purpose of the event was to raise funds for the Spike Community Project in Charlotteville. The Vagrant's Casual Ward, also known as The Spike, is the last remaining building from the former St Luke's Hospital site in Warren Road. Local residents fought a long battle to save this historic building from demolition and have it converted into a community facility.

One race, open to all, attracted gentlemen dressed in various modes of attire. Bringing up the rear is well-known Guildfordian Richard Bergman, who seems to be chasing a criminal to the finishing line.

There were also well-contested races by children from local schools. The children had no problems running over the High Street's granite setts, as long as they didn't drop their pancake!

The Guildford Fire Brigade also entered into the spirit of the occasion with a team relay race. It was a novelty to watch firemen flipping pancakes dressed in their heavy protective clothing and carrying their breathing apparatus!

ROYAL SURREY COUNTY HOSPITAL RALLY

In November 2006 a rally was held in the High Street to show public support for the Save the Royal Surrey County Hospital Appeal. It drew a crowd of between 5,000 and 6,000. Rumours that the hospital's A&E department was threatened with closure, or even worse that the main hospital might be shut down, shocked the people of Guildford and surrounding towns and villages who rely on the hospital.

Among the speakers addressing the assembled mass, from the steps of Holy Trinity Church, were Professor Richard Marks, a well-respected consultant surgeon at the Royal Surrey County Hospital for many years, Anne Milton MP and Guildford former MP Sue Doughty. Holding the microphone, speaking to a receptive audience, is Surrey County Councillor Sarah di Capia.

People came to Guildford from far and wide to protest against the prospect of losing their local hospital. This group had travelled from the Haslemere area.

Even current patients attended to show their support, as well as younger members of the community who were made aware of the importance of keeping their local hospital.

THE PASSION PLAY

Many different events and facets of Guildford life take place in the High Street. Wintershall Players, who are based on the Wintershall Estate near Bramley, have performed *Life of Christ* at Wintershall since the year 2000. It was meant to be a one-off event for the Millennium celebrations, but it proved to be so popular that they now hold performances every year. The religious play has attracted over 100,000 people since the first year, and there are up to 3,000 spectators on each day. In recent years, on Easter Saturday, Wintershall Players have given an open-air performance of *The Passion*, making use of the length of the High Street. Shoppers have had the opportunity to see this section of the *Life of Christ* production, which is staged at Wintershall later on in the summer. *The Passion* play begins with the trial of Jesus, performed at the junction with Quarry Street.

As performers move up the street the audience are invited to join them and walk to Calvary to witness a crucifixion.

With the performers wearing microphones and speakers lining the street, everybody is able to follow as the play changes location and the actors arrive at Holy Trinity Church.

The crucifixion tableau is staged against the church's north wall.

The crowd are quiet as this very moving scene of Jesus on the cross and Mary dropping to her knees in despair is played out.

Onlookers remain silent as the play moves on, and the body of Jesus is carried to a small cave that has been constructed nearby. A stone is then rolled across the entrance to seal the tomb.

Later, when the stone is rolled back, it reveals an empty cave.

This excellent play ends on the steps of Holy Trinity Church. It is a free performance, much enjoyed and appreciated by Saturday shoppers in the High Street, and the large crowd give the actors rapturous applause.

BUSKERS IN HIGH STREET

Street entertainment brightens any town centre, and Guildford is no exception. Here are well-respected group *Stringfever* busking in 2005. They play their own style of classical music. The band comprises brothers Giles, Ralph and Neil Broadbent, and their cousin Graham. They claim to be the world's first 'genetically modified' string quartet. Since the early days of busking on Guildford's streets, they have performed in venues such as The Dorchester, Grosvenor House, Hilton Hotels in London and Shelborne Hotel in Dublin. In 2006 the band entertained on board *Queen Mary II*, sailing between Barbados and New York. If you want to make it in the music world, Guildford is a good place to start!

These 'living statues' fascinate all ages, and the children especially enjoy their 'non-performance'.

GUILDFORD'S TWIN

The town band from the City of Freiberg in Germany visited Guildford in October 2004 as part of the link between the twin towns. Freiberg, which is situated in south-west Germany and has a population of over 210,000, was twinned with Guildford in 1979. It is an historic city with a 700-year-old cathedral and a university population of approximately 25,000, which was founded in 1457. There is a Guildford–Freiberg Association that promotes the bonds between the two towns and encourages exchange visits and other links between schools, local businesses and other groups in the town keen to participate.

The pedestrianized High Street makes an ideal venue for open-air entertainment, which can suit many different tastes and styles. Here, The Huckleberries perform during a Heritage Open Day in 2006.

TOWN CENTRE CYCLE RACES

Each year, during the town's summer festival, top-class cycle racing takes place around Guildford town centre. The event is organised by Charlotteville Cycling Club, which was founded in 1903 near to the High Street, in the community of Charlotteville.

There are races for the Under-12s and older local riders, and then the excitement increases when the next races contain national and international competitors. The number of laps covered on this testing circuit varies according to the ability of the riders taking part. Starting in High Street, riders travel down into North Street, up Market Street and then back up the granite setts of High Street to the finish line in front of Abbot's Hospital.

FARMERS' MARKET IN HIGH STREET

With High Street pedestrianised during the daytime, it has opened up numerous opportunities for new enterprises and events to use the street. One that has become very popular, on the first Tuesday of each month, is the farmers' market.

Shoppers can now sample fresh produce, plants and crafts offered by small local businesses from all over the county. The market attracts customers onto the High Street to browse the many stalls, and it is a lively, bustling monthly event.

REMEMBRANCE SUNDAY IN HIGH STREET

Organisation of ceremonial occasions in Guildford is second to none; however, on Remembrance Sunday 2005 a car parked outside Holy Trinity Church could have changed all that. Within 25 minutes, the mayor and other dignitaries were due to assemble on this very spot to receive a march past by various groups from the Guildford area. Fortunately, the prompt action taken by Surrey Constabulary to remove the offending vehicle avoided any embarrassment on this occasion.

The procession left the Guildhall on time, led by town crier Mr David Peters, for the short walk up the High Street to Holy Trinity Church for the Remembrance Day Service.

Mayor Tamsey Baker is seen here having a word with Guildford's Member of Parliament, Anne Milton, before the various groups marched past them down the High Street. Bill and Doreen Bellerby, both previous mayors of Guildford, are standing to the left wearing their blue Freedom of the Borough robes.

Leading the parade was Guildford's Friary Brass Band, carrying on with the name of the long gone Friary Brewery Band. Following them were representatives from the Armed Forces Veterans Associations, and cadets from the army, navy and air force also took part.

REMEMBRANCE SUNDAY IN THE CASTLE GROUNDS

After the church service, a civic procession made its way to the war memorial in the castle grounds. There, the mayor paid her respects and laid a wreath – the first of many to be laid by dignitaries and local people.

A member of the British Legion is present every year to deliver the exhortation.

'When you go home, tell them of us and say,
For your tomorrows these gave their today.'

John Maxwell Edmonds.

'They went with songs to the battle, they were young
Straight of limb, true of eye, steady and aglow
They were staunch to the end against odds encountered
They fell with their faces to the foe.

They shall grow not old, as we that are left grow old
Age shall not weary them, nor the years condemn
At the going down of the sun and in the morning
We will remember them.'

Laurence Binyon.

CASTLE GROUNDS

Guildford's War Memorial to men from the town who lost their lives in World War One was erected in 1921 and designed by a local man, Mr F.J. Hodgson. 'Freddie' Hodgson involved himself very much in the life of the town, especially with the football club. He became chairman of Guildford City FC in the 1920s and later president of the club until his death in 1970.

Lt General Sir Edmund Elles officiated at the unveiling of the memorial on Sunday 6 November 1921, and Lord Bishop of Winchester, The Right Reverend Dr Talbot, carried out the dedication. Guildford did not have its own bishop until the enthronement of John Harold Greig as the first Lord Bishop of Guildford in Holy Trinity Church on 12 July 1927.

The Castle Keep underwent major conservation work during 2003–04, mostly funded by Guildford Borough Council. English Heritage helped with a grant of £100,000 towards the project's total cost, which reached £750,000 after more than a year of restoration work. During the work, one of the interesting discoveries was a gap between the walls that turned out to be a mediaeval garderobe, which today we would call a toilet. This indicates that for a time the keep functioned as a residence of some importance and was not only used for defensive purposes. The main castle, which covered a march larger area than the grounds we see today, was probably a fairly significant royal residence during the 12th and 13th centuries.

With the transformation of the keep, there came a name change. When the 12th-century tower was built it would, apparently, have been referred to as the Great Tower, though it had been known as the keep since Elizabethan times. For over 60 years the author has recognised it as the Castle Keep and will still use this name for continuity's sake. The original height of the tower is indicated by new rendering, which has been applied to the outside of the building during the conservation work. This restoration has removed previous attempts to preserve the keep in past centuries, which may not have been of the highest standard and more detrimental than beneficial. The Castle Keep, sitting on its motte, and the beautifully kept gardens are a joy to visit and one of the town's real treasures. With the reopening of this ancient royal residence in June 2004, it would have been hugely symbolic if our reigning monarch could have attended the ceremony. The queen was, however, destined to visit Guildford two years later for another ancient ceremony, which can be seen on page 118.

There is now a roof on the Castle Keep for the first time in about 350 years, and with the construction of an oak floor at the first-floor level, there is an entirely different experience and atmosphere when visiting the keep today. Instead of being open to the elements, there is now more to awaken your interest and imagination as to what it had been like in its prime over 700 years ago.

From the rooftop observation area, the town opens up around you. Looking across the rooftops towards Sydenham Road, the tower of Holy Trinity Church and cupolas of Abbot's Hospital can be seen. Now the restoration is complete, the once royal residence hopefully has many more years to enthral the visitor with its history and stories of previous kings and queens who stayed at Guildford Castle.

THE QUEEN'S VISIT, 2006

One event eagerly awaited was the visit from Her Majesty The Queen to the Guildford Cathedral in 2006 – the year of her 80th birthday. Her Majesty came to distribute Maundy Money in a ceremony at the cathedral. It being her 80th birthday, 80 retired men and 80 retired women received commemorative coins, which had a total face value of 80 pence. After the ceremony, the Queen, accompanied by Prince Philip, had lunch with Mayor Tamsey Baker at the Guildhall. Alighting from the royal Bentley near Swan Lane in the High Street, the couple strolled up the hill, talking to the flag-waving crowds of well-wishers, who broke out into spontaneous choruses of *Happy Birthday*.

The Queen received numerous bouquets of flowers and birthday cards from the crowds. She was happy to speak to as many people as possible, and the lucky ones were able to have a chat and express their best wishes for her 80th birthday.

As Her Majesty arrived outside the Guildhall, a lady in the crowd who had been waiting since 7am told the Queen that she was also 80 years old and presented her with a birthday card. Her Majesty looked genuinely appreciative of the lady's efforts.

Prince Philip seemed to be enjoying himself as well, and he was a big hit with the ladies.

The Queen and Duke of Edinburgh inspected Guildford's traditional plum cake, which is always presented to reigning monarchs when they visit the town.

A rather apprehensive-looking young boy is given reassurance and last instructions before he meets the Queen and presents her with a bouquet outside the Guildhall.

Before leaving the crowded High Street to dine with the mayor and guests inside the historic building, the young boy, from 1st Guildford Company of The Boys' Brigade, finally has his big moment and presents Her Majesty with the bouquet of flowers.

When the Queen entered the Guildhall to have lunch, the royal ensign was raised above its Bell Tower.

THE BOYS' BRIGADE

The Guildford Boys' Brigade is part of an organisation that has troops throughout Britain. Sir William A. Smith, a Baptist, founded The Boys' Brigade when he formed a company of 30 boys in Glasgow in 1883. This makes it the oldest national club for boys in the country. In 1939 the 1st Guildford Company held their meetings at the Baptist Church in Commercial Road, which unfortunately is no longer there. It was demolished in 1974, and the empty space is still awaiting a new development to this day. This photograph shows 1st Guildford's band heading a parade through the town centre in 1939. The drummer boys leading the group are William Pollard in the centre, Norman Beer on the right side and a young lad named Clark on the left. The captain of the troop, Fred Over, is the man playing the trumpet, while on bass drum is Vivian Over and Frank Over is on the cymbals. Following on behind in the parade is 9th Guildford Scout Troop with their leader, Mr Jeffreys, marching up front.

One activity The Boys' Brigade felt very strongly about was instructing its members in first aid. In 1937 William Pollard received this certificate for his achievements in ambulance work and first aid. William went on to spend his working life at his Guildford family's plumbing and heating business, Pollard Bros. When his father and two uncles retired, he and his brother Godfrey, better known as Charlie, managed the firm, which their grandfather had started in the town in 1896.

HIGH STREET PARADES

This proud group of smartly turned-out young lads are from Holy Trinity and St Mary's School, and they marched down High Street in 1897 as part of the celebrations for Queen Victoria's Diamond Jubilee. The fact that the boys were carrying replica rifles would not have caused a stir in Victorian times as it would today. Many of these boys were probably already shooting rabbits and pigeons in the woods and fields around the town.

On their return to Guildford in April 1902, after two years' service in South Africa, the 3rd Battalion of The Queen's Royal West Surrey Militia were given a hearty reception from the people of their hometown. The men were met at the railway station by the mayor, corporation and many military officers. After the parade, they were invited to dine in the Drill Hall in upper High Street, where they also received their service medals. The Drill Hall was situated on the corner of High Street and Alexander Terrace, opposite The White Horse Hotel. At the time, the 24th Surrey Rifle Volunteers had it as their base. Later, the building became a skating rink, and then in 1924 Puttock's Garage took over the site. After their ceremonial duties in 1902, the soldiers returned to their barracks in Stoughton.

The military had their army barracks in Guildford for over 100 years. Before the 1870s the area at the lower end of North Street, backing on to the River Wey, was the location of a town centre Victorian barracks, but then in 1876 Stoughton became the preferred area for a new barracks. Soldiers regularly paraded through the town's streets to mark special occasions. This group of soldiers marched up High Street in 1911; however, they had come from Aldershot on this particular occasion.

After the discipline of the ceremonials, these troops were allowed to relax at Pewley Fort. Among the dignitaries accompanying them at Pewley were Frank Lasham, standing on the far left, who in 1894 had worked with others to acquire Woodbridge Road sports ground for the town. On his left is Fredrick Elsley who acted as Guildford Institute's librarian from 1896 until 1944. Both men were involved in many aspects of Guildford life, including amateur theatre groups, sports clubs, and each served as president of Guildford Natural History and Literary Society.

SURREY RIFLE CLUBS AT NEWLANDS CORNER

With the end of the Boar War in 1902 and the beginning of World War One, there was always a threat of a possible invasion from Europe of some kind or other. In July 1906 the Surrey Rifle Club staged its fifth Field Day at Newlands Corner, just a few miles from Guildford. The event involved a competition between rifle clubs from different districts around Guildford.

The concept was that there was a division of a German invading army at Aldershot, and the regular, organised opposition to the invasion was over. Each club had to show its skills as a roving band of English irregular riflemen acting as 'commandos' and then cause as much trouble as possible for the enemy – on their bikes?

CHURCH SERVICE AT NEWLANDS CORNER

The first Bishop of Guildford, John Harold Greig, was a firm believer in taking church services out to the people. This photograph clearly illustrates the success of this belief. A large gathering of local people came together in the late 1920s to form his congregation on the slopes of Newlands Corner.

Newlands Corner is only about a mile from the centre of Guildford and is a favourite walk for keen ramblers from the town or just a short drive to get to for the less energetic. From this vantage point on the North Downs, the view takes in Albury Park and beyond. On a clear day you can see the South Downs.

THE MYSTERY OF AGATHA CHRISTIE

In early December 1926 Newlands Corner became the centre of a mystery that gripped the whole nation. The car belonging to well-known author Agatha Christie was found abandoned there, and she had vanished. Deputy Chief Constable Supt Kenward of Surrey Police took charge of the case and organised a thorough search of the area between Merrow and Shere. He was convinced there was a serious crime to investigate. Local police and about 2,000 volunteers from around Guildford took part in the operation of combing the countryside for Mrs Christie's body.

Beaters worked in woods and through scrubland looking for clues. It so happened that a few days earlier, Agatha Christie's husband Archie had left her for his mistress Nancy Neele, and they were staying in Hurtmore near Godalming with friends. Why had she driven from her home at Sunningdale in Berkshire to Newlands Corner in Surrey – a journey of about 14 miles? Her car's handbrake had been left off and its headlights were left on. Mrs Christie's travelling case and coat were found inside the car. Had she intended to commit suicide or had there been a murder? It was like something out of the pages of one of her novels!

The police dragged the Silent Pool, and a tremendous amount of time and effort went into the search for Mrs Christie by Surrey Police and the general public. On Sunday 12 December 1926, over a week after she went missing, thousands of people joined in the search, which had spread to Albury and Chilworth, and then almost to Dorking. They drew a blank. It seemed only Supt Kenward believed he would still find a body, and he was convinced she had been murdered.

This photograph of the Silent Pool was taken three years earlier in 1923 on a very rare occasion when the spring that feeds the pool dried up.

On the evening of Sunday 12 December, two people in Harrogate contacted Yorkshire Police to inform them that a woman closely resembling the missing Mrs Christie was staying at the Harrogate Hydro Hotel. The next day, West Riding Police observed the guest calling herself 'Mrs Teresa Neele' and were convinced they had found the missing novelist. They informed Supt Kenward that Mrs Christie had travelled to Yorkshire and booked into the hotel. He chose not to believe them and continued his search for a body. He planned the next search for Wednesday 15 December; however, on the Tuesday her husband travelled north and identified that this lady was indeed his wife. Mrs Christie claimed to be suffering from amnesia. Supt Kenward had no choice but to call off the search, and Mrs Christie was taken to her sister's home near Manchester to 'recuperate'. Two distinguished doctors, who examined her at the time, both agreed she had suffered amnesia.

There are many theories as to what exactly happened to Agatha Christie that December. The most popular conjecture is that she staged the entire theatrical event to humiliate her wayward husband. It is generally assumed that she abandoned her car at Newlands Corner, then walked to Clandon Station and caught a train to London. There she stayed the night with an old friend, and in the morning she continued her journey north by train to Harrogate. Surely it can be no coincidence that she registered as a 'Mrs Neele' at the hotel, Neele being the surname of her husband's mistress?

NEWLANDS CORNER

Over the decades, Newlands Corner has always appealed to people as a place to visit for its great views, fresh air, good walks and peaceful surroundings. In 1927 maybe more people than usual visited this beauty spot because of the events of the December before, intrigued to see the spot where Agatha Christie left her car. In this photograph of 1927, St Martha's Chapel's tower can just be seen across the valley at the top of St Martha's Hill. Today, mature trees that envelop the hillside obscure this same view.

St Martha's rounded hill is an interesting spot. Why build a chapel on such a steep hill, a fair distance from the nearest village or hamlet? It is reasonably certain that Druids considered this hilltop a holy place and worshipped here many centuries ago. It is quite possible that human sacrifices took place here too. If, in fact, early Christians did suffer persecution, the first chapel built on the site by the Saxons was most likely dedicated to their memory. In later years, pilgrims on their way to Winchester and Canterbury would have climbed the hill to pray for these martyrs at St Martha's Chapel. With the Dissolution of the Monasteries in 1538, the building fell into disrepair. The chapel we see today was built in 1848.

St Martha's Chapel

When walkers use the track from Halfpenny Lane through the trees to the chapel today, they follow in the footsteps of travellers who have passed this way for over 2,000 years. In recent years, the chapel's burial ground has become the last resting place for at least two well-known Guildford residents. Yvonne Arnaud, a great actress and musician, has her ashes scattered here. She spent her last few years living in Guildford, and the town's theatre is named after her, although she never performed there herself. Also, Sir George Edwards, a world-renowned aircraft designer who lived in White Lane for about 40 years, is buried in the churchyard. Sir George was involved in the development of jet aircraft, including the Valient, the Viscount and the sublime Concorde. A memorial service was held at Guildford Cathedral in 2003 in his honour and was attended by the Duke of Kent, former Prime Minister John Major and Sir Dennis Rooke who represented the queen. If you visit Brooklands Museum near Weybridge you will see, among other things, his hat in a display cabinet as part of the exhibition inside the Concorde, which has been reconstructed there.

This wartime postcard was probably issued in 1940–41, and it was most likely part of a rallying call for Home Guard volunteers. They were also produced for other areas, complete with their own local landmark as the centrepiece. St Martha's Chapel, with its exceptional location, has held the affections of generations of Guildfordians. One of the most popular walks from the town includes a climb up through Chantry Wood to the chapel and then returning over Pewley Downs. The chapel has a 'sound' connection with the town centre, as for a number of years its old bell rang out over the town from the Guildhall bell tower.

131

THE GUILDHALL BELL

In 1931 the eventful life of the former St Martha's Chapel bell finally ended when a crack appeared and it needed to be replaced. The bell had not only chimed for the Guildhall clock, but it was also rung in the event of an emergency to call the fire brigade, which had its horses and appliances based in North Street during the 1800s and early 1900s.

This ancient bell may not be heard any more, but it can still be seen as it is now housed on the ground floor of the Guildhall. This photograph shows the ingenious apparatus made by H. Ashenden's workmen to lower the bell to the ground in 1931.

THE GUILDHALL CLOCK

Here is an even more elaborate construction used to work on the clock face. One wonders how the health and safety inspectors would view this resourcefulness nowadays. Earlier in 1931, urgent repairs to the famous clock were necessary. The work cost the town council a princely sum of £78. During World War Two the clock had to be removed again, and this time it was for safekeeping, in case it suffered bomb damage. It was hidden in a secret location, where it remained until the hostilities ended. After the war many people speculated that this secret hiding place could well have been in the crypt of the unfinished cathedral on Stag Hill.

GATES FIRE

In the early hours of 17 June 1916, the Guildhall's bell would have been rung to sound the alarm for a fire at the Gates grocery shop in the High Street, next door to the Three Pigeons public house.

The fire started in a storeroom at the rear of the building. It also spread to the Three Pigeons, which required extensive rebuilding work.

Gates was completely destroyed. In the mid-1880s Mr Gates senior, who sold wines and spirits as well as groceries, ran the business. When his sons, who were strictly teetotal, inherited the business they ceased selling alcohol. The story goes that they agreed to pour all the wines and spirits out on to the street. From this small shop in Guildford, Cow and Gate evolved, which eventually became Uni-Gate.

The next building down the street was the historic Abbot's Hospital, and the fire could very well have affected it.

Thankfully, only a small building attached to Abbot's Hospital was damaged, and the main building escaped any structural harm.

135

THE BRITANNIA FIRE

Four years before the Gates fire, another town fire could have resulted in loss of life. The blaze at the Britannia public house, situated by the river at Millmead, also started in the early hours and completely wrecked the building. In the 1800s and early 1900s the Britannia Beerhouse, its name at that time, was constructed of wood. On the night of 21 September 1912 a fire swept through the building endangering the lives of the landlord, Arthur Duffell, his wife and their child. They owed their survival to their pet dog, a fox terrier named Nell, who sounded the alarm. Mr Duffell was awoken at about 3am by the frantic barking of the dog. Nell was only four or five months old and was so close to their child that she was allowed to sleep in its cot at night, which was situated beside Mr Duffell's bed. On waking, Mr Duffell opened the bedroom door to be met by a great wall of flames. He managed to help his wife and child out of the bedroom window on to the scullery roof, and then he returned to rescue Nell. All four of them safely reached the ground, and Nell received a shield and medal from Spratt's Canine Heroes League.

On the left-hand side of this picture you can see the Britannia during the floods of 1900, when the river overflowed and damaged these Millmead properties. Friary Holyroyd and Healy, the brewery who leased the building, wanted to rebuild the Britannia as it was before the fire, but Guildford Corporation refused to allow a timber reconstruction and insisted on a brick building, which stands today at Millmead. How the original fire started was a mystery. Mr Duffell's only suggestion was that a cigarette had been thrown down in the bar and had been left smouldering on the floor.

For a few years, from the late 1990s until 2003, the owners of the pub, in their wisdom, renamed it Scruffy Murphy's, but in 2003 it reverted to its original name.

WHITE'S FIRE

Between September 1912 and June 1916 there were at least four major fires in the centre of Guildford. The Britannia public house, the Reeks store, the Gates shop and, on the afternoon of 24 June 1914, White and Son's High Street store were gutted by fire. The White and Son's property was completely destroyed and required extensive rebuilding.

Not only did the original White and Son's building have an attractive High Street frontage, but also some of its interior was comparable to a country house.

It is an 'ill wind', as they say, and the loss of White and Son's business premise turned out to be Guildford shoppers' gain. The salvage sale of goods on 20 July attracted an unprecedented number of customers for a cut-price bonanza of items, including raincoats and umbrellas selling for one shilling (five pence) each. I wonder if anyone was looking for a new hat that day? White and Son's store reopened and traded until the 1960s when it was demolished, and Bovis Builders erected the new Marks & Spencer store.

Similar to Marks & Spencer, W.E. White and Son's store extended through from High Street to North Street. It could have been referred to as either 62–63–64 High Street or 45–46 North Street.

THE LION HOTEL

The next building from White and Son's on the High Street was the Lion Hotel, which changed its name to White Lion in later years. In 1902 coach and horses re-enacted a scene from bygone days, when up to 20 coaches passed through the town usually en route between London and Southampton or Portsmouth. The coaches had grand names such as *Night Rocket*, *Royal Blue*, *Star*, *Red Rover*, *Rocket Union* and *Tantivy*. Guildford's first coach of the day, *Royal William*, passed through at 10.30am on its way to Southampton. Probably the last arrival would have been the *Portsmouth Mail*, which left London at 8pm and pulled in the Crown Hotel's yard (now NatWest Bank) shortly after midnight.

Guildford was in the ideal position for the coaches' overnight stop, but with the coming of the rail in 1845 there was a steady decline in coach business for all of Guildford's hotels. The last coach passed through the town in 1849. In 1902 the Lion Hotel had extensive alterations and additions, so we must assume the management were optimistic about future business. The Lion Hotel was a popular venue for dinner dances and society meetings. In the early 1900s there were enough stalls and loose boxes for no less than 60 horses, and with the changing times a special motor and cycle house was built.

On arrival, guests would immediately gain a sense of the hotel's elegance and style from its ornate entrance hall. The Lion Hotel managed to attract visitors right up until its closure and demolition in 1957. Surrey's cricket team regularly stayed there in the 1950s, when playing their annual matches at Woodbridge Road Sports Ground. Maybe the Bedser twins, Alec and Eric, were exceptions as they probably returned to their home in Woking.

This is the coffee lounge, and even with the alterations in 1902 we can assume that this room remained the same. Changes did include 30 new bedrooms 'with easy access to bathrooms and lavatories'. This meant a short walk along the corridor, but a few rooms did have en-suite facilities and a sitting room. Another luxury amenity the hotel offered their guests was a 'hotel handsomely lighted by electricity'. It has to be remembered that in 1902 the majority of homes would have been dependent on gas lighting or even oil lamps.

THE ANGEL HOTEL

With the demise of the Lion Hotel, there remains only one of the original High Street coaching inns in the 21st century. The Angel Hotel is in fact the oldest of the inns, dating back to at least 1527.

There have been times when the Angel could well have followed the fate of Guildford's other historic inns. On 1 January 1886 a fire occurred in the billiard room. If it had not been for the alertness of members of staff who discovered the fire at 6am and the nearness of the Guildford Fire Brigade's engine shed in North Street, one of the town's oldest buildings could have been lost forever. It is very possible that some of the men in this 1883 photograph attended the fire at the Angel and helped save such an important part of Guildford's heritage.

It is said that the High Street water hydrants were so powerful that the force of the water putting out the fire in the billiard room carried a billiard ball through the roof, and it landed in Swan Lane some 25 yards away. The heat from the fire stopped the Act of Parliament clock, which was situated on the wall of the hall staircase. These clocks were introduced in 1797 when William Pitt, The Younger, placed a tax on clocks and watches that were for personal use. Clocks that were installed in prominent positions where the public had access to them, which included inns, avoided the tax. Consequently, they became known as Act of Parliament clocks. In this 1920s photograph, the internal windows of the lounge bar can be seen on the right-hand side. Note the number of elaborate plant-pot arrangements in the hall and on the staircase.

This 2004 photograph shows the hall with the lounge bar windows removed and the Parliament clock minus its base. In 1989, when the hotel changed hands, the clock was removed and taken away. Guildford Borough Council requested its return, but when this was refused they took enforcement action. Eventually, the clock was returned to its rightful home at the Angel.

This is the lounge bar showing the internal lead-light windows. For many years, the pleasant bar was a popular lunchtime meeting place for the local business community and for people shopping in the town.

By the late 1980s this bar area had been converted into a quiet sitting room for hotel residents only.

When renovation works were carried out in around 1870, workmen had problems finding a suitable angel's head to fix over the entrance archway. One of the workmen, Mr Mills, a plasterer, came up with a novel idea. He took a clay moulding from a monument in Holy Trinity Churchyard, and from this he made an angel's head, which can still be seen above the arch today.

In October 1989 Mr Corcoran, the hotel's general manager, locked the front door of the Angel Hotel for what looked likely to be the last time. Trusthouse Forte had sold the hotel to Grosvenor Properties Ltd. There was talk of turning the site into a shopping mall or offices, but the council and townspeople rallied in protest against this scheme. Grosvenor then decided to lease the property to County Catering and Leisure, and the hotel reopened once again as the Angel in 1992.

Back in 1964 Trusthouse Forte had great plans for the Angel Hotel. They converted the undercroft, which had acted as a junk room, into a new luxury bar as part of their £120,000 facelift project. There was going to be room for about 40 people in the bar. The ancient stone walls were left unpainted and the floor uncovered. Seats ringed the wall, and illumination came from light sets in the Gothic ceiling alcoves. Air conditioning and central heating were installed. They hoped that the bar would attract wealthy middle-class clients; 'let's hope the students will keep away,' a hotel official was heard to say at the time.

It was not long before the undercroft became the Crypt Restaurant. There is no evidence that the undercroft ever had any connections with religious worship or that there were any secret tunnels, as was often rumoured. It is a 13th-century construction, as is the undercroft on the opposite side of High Street. Both were probably used as shops, and the owners' living quarters would have been at ground level.

Angel Gate, which is an ancient public right of way, can be viewed here in 1960, and this picture shows that the hotel had retained the sign for the ostler's quarters on the right. There may not have been a great deal for an ostler to do in the 1960s, but during the days of the horse-drawn carriage his job was to look after the guests' horses and was one of the most important services offered by the hotel for their travelling clientele.

In the 1960s the courtyard area was still reserved for guest parking, albeit of the four-wheeled variety rather than the four-legged. Nowadays the courtyard is utilised by the town's shoppers, with alfresco tables and chairs for them to take a break, relax and enjoy refreshments. A florist shop now trades from the old ostler's quarters.

Today's Angel Hotel is fulfilling the business that it has carried out for centuries – caring for the travelling public. It was touch-and-go in 1989, but now it is one of the premium hotels in the south east of England. If it had not been for the Guildford Borough Council standing firm at that time, and with support from The Guildford Society, there would be shops and offices on this site today; however, where High Street properties are concerned there could always be another attempt to convert the Angel Hotel into a department store.

When writing about the Angel Hotel, the haunted bedroom must at least have a short mention. Guests over many years have reported seeing a reflection of a man in military uniform staring back at them from a large wardrobe mirror. Petula Clark, the singer, apparently saw him. Roger Moore, the actor, stayed at the hotel in 1973, and while occupying bedroom one he allegedly saw a white figure moving around the room. Maybe a soldier suffered a violent death centuries ago in this very room?

TUNSGATE

Apparently, Guildford has numerous ghosts in the town centre, and it seems that another one pops up every year. Christopher Slaughterford is said to haunt the Tunsgate area. He was the last man to be executed in Guildford town centre. He was hanged from a scaffold erected in High Street at the Three Tuns Inn in 1709.

Tunsgate arch, site of the Three Tuns, is now a pleasant part of the town centre. It seems appropriate that flowers are sold under the arch. Christopher Slaughterford was convicted of murdering his sweetheart Jane Young in the grounds of Loseley Park, but up to the very end he denied that he committed the dastardly deed.

JUSTICE AND PUNISHMENT

Justice was most certainly harsh in the 1700s. Guildford's Jail, built in 1604, was situated opposite St Mary's Church in Quarry Street. This building replaced the Castle Keep as a place of detention. It served the town for over 200 years. A report on Guildford's Jail in 1788 painted an appalling picture of the place and the treatment of its prisoners. It stated that there were eight prisoners in the jail, which had not been whitewashed for many years and only had a small day room for men and women to share and, in the words of the report, 'with a pig stye in the corner'. They were allowed

15 ounces each of badly baked bread a day. In 1818 another report stated that there were 35 prisoners in the jail, but there had been as many as 100. Prisoners complained of the cold and that fever was rife. There was not any work for the inmates to do, apart from moving gravel in small buckets from one end of the yard to the other and then back again.

It was from Guildford Jail in 1818 that criminals Chernell and Chalcroft were taken, by cart, to a meadow in Godalming to be hanged in the presence of an enormous crowd. William Elkins, mayor of Guildford in 1824 and 1830, was known as Billy Whip because during his time in office the last prisoner was whipped all the way up High Street tied to a cart. Elkins is buried in Holy Trinity Churchyard. He is also remembered by a short ditty:

'Billy the Whip, Billy Bung
From a grocer he was sprung
To a brewer he was bound
Then got mayor of Guildford Town.'

One of many forms of punishment inflicted on rogues and vagabonds in the 1700s was the ducking stool. In a little garden bordering the River Wey at Millmead, where the water is deepest and it enters the Town Mill, a large 12-foot high post was fixed. The post had a long mortise not far from its top. A beam with a chair fixed to it moved up and down for the 'ducking of scolds'. It was also considered an appropriate procedure to nearly drown a woman who was in the habit of 'speaking her mind'!

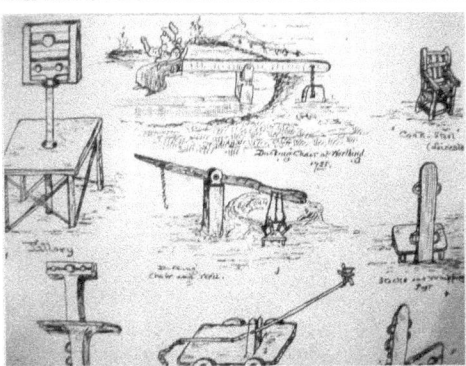

These other ducking stools were featured in an 1883 *Building News* article on punishment in the Middle Ages. Any number of these contraptions could possibly have been used on the people of Guildford who misbehaved.

THE TOWN MILLS

The Town Mill as we know it today is completely different from the scene that 18th-century Guildfordians were familiar with. At that time, there were three water mills driving the grain-grinding stones at Millmead, as illustrated in Thomas Russell's sketch, *c*.1750. In 1701 a water-driven turbine was installed to pump water to a reservoir at the foot of Pewley Hill.

The wood structures gave way to a new brick building in 1771, which was extended in the 1860s. Milling ceased in 1894, but water continued to be pumped up to the reservoir at Pewley.

THE TOWN'S WATER SUPPLY

The original reservoir at Pewley was constructed in 1850, and it supplied water to the town centre. Guildford was rapidly expanding in the 1860s, with houses being built further out and higher up the hills around the town. This one reservoir soon became inadequate for the town's water needs.

The bricks used to construct the reservoir came from Guildford's run-down jail building, which had been demolished in the early 1800s. A much larger reservoir was required, and this had to be built at the top of Pewley Hill. When this came on flow, it supplemented the original reservoir until the old construction was eventually dismantled in March 1925.

Henry Peak, architect of the project and borough surveyor, has already been mentioned, as he was the mastermind behind the laying of the High Street granite setts. In this old photograph he can be seen wearing a top hat, standing on the roof of the unfinished reservoir, talking to another man. It is interesting to observe that most of the men are wearing top hats, so we might conclude that this was the 'topping out' ceremony in 1866.

The last water-driven turbine was eventually removed from the Toll House in 1990, after sitting in the millstream for some 60 years. Removing the turbine, which weighed two tonnes, turned out to be no easy undertaking. A crane lifted it through the roof and then placed it on a waiting lorry, which then transported it to a workshop for restoration.

151

After restoring one of Surrey's few remaining water turbines, Guildford Borough Council, in partnership with The National Trust, moved it to Dapdune Wharf, where they put it on display. The National Trust has displayed a diagram explaining the workings of the turbine.

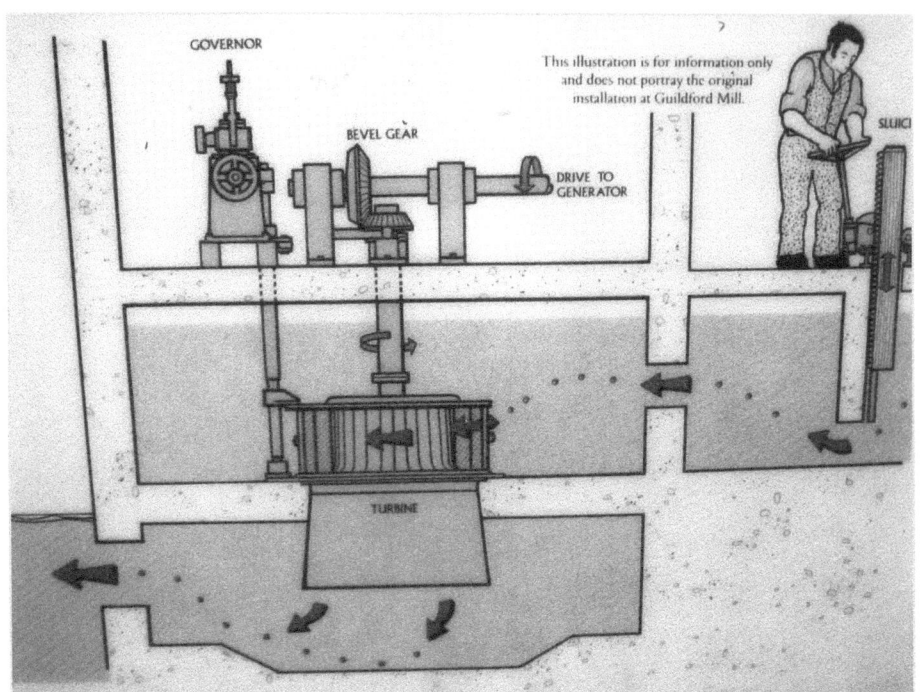

The Toll House at Millmead has now become the home for a new turbine, this time to generate hydro-electric power. Mayor Angela Gunning officially opened the project in September 2006. Electricity generated by the scheme will help power council buildings, and any surplus will enter the National Grid. The original Toll House building collected bargemen's toll charges that were levied on their cargoes when using the Wey Navigation.

THE RIVER THROUGH THE TOWN CENTRE

Crooke's Brewery, on the left, brewed beer alongside the River Wey for over 100 years until 1929, when it eventually ceased trading. At the time it owned 25 fully-licensed houses in local towns and villages. A treadwheel crane for loading and unloading river barge goods is situated next to the old sailing barge, seen tied up at the town wharf. This treadwheel has been preserved and is the only feature that survives today from this early photograph.

Farnham Road bus station occupied the brewery land from 1950 until the early 1980s when the town's bus station moved to the other side of the new Friary Shopping Centre. The site is currently used as a car park. For over 25 years, various ideas have been put forward to enhance the area and make this prime riverside location a focal point for the town. Currently there are plans to build a cultural centre with a new town library and art gallery. This section of the beautiful River Wey could once again come alive and be utilised and enjoyed by the people of Guildford.

RIVER WEY BOAT FESTIVAL, 2002

A river is an important lifeblood and crucial to any town, and Guildford's relationship with the River Wey is no different. In recent years the river has become a great asset for leisure and recreation. Over 100 boats took part in the Guildford Festival Boat Gathering in July 2002. The theme that year was the queen's Golden Jubilee.

People's ingenuity and creativity holds no bounds! This boat was decorated as the royal train. The excitement was unrestrained at this very moment, as the engine had just produced smoke from its chimney for the first time.

LIONS CLUB RAFT RACE, 2003

Enthusiastic crowds lined the riverbanks through the town centre in July 2003 for the annual Guildford Lions Club charity raft race. The 2.5km course from Millmead to the Waterside Centre at Stoke took the homemade, custom-built rafts between 25 and 90 minutes, braving the barrage of water bombs and flour thrown from the river bank and bridges along the route by rival team members.

The Royal Surrey County Hospital's entry was one of 38 that entered into the spirit of the event. Over 200 people were involved with the rafts on the river that day, and everybody was in it to win it.

LIONS CLUB RAFT RACE, 2007

Four years later, and the determination and competitive nature of the race prevailed. Most rafts reached Dapdune Wharf without too much distress and in one piece. Jason and the Argonauts are seen here speeding past Guildford Sea Cadets' headquarters, over halfway to the finish line at the Weyside Centre, here in the 2007 race.

A mother and her six cygnets watch on, bemused about the sudden rush of human activity that is disturbing the usual peace and quiet of the Woodbridge Meadows stretch of the river.

Here is the last raft arriving at the finish line, with a little helpful assistance from a thoughtful couple passing in a motor launch. Who says this is cheating?

The race-weary crew eventually make it to dry land, one and a half hours after leaving Millmead. Their spirits were not dampened; at least their efforts included a traditionally constructed raft, which just about made it intact. The fastest time on the day for the 2.5km course was 21 minutes, but it is the taking part that counts.

RIVER WEY BRIDGES

On the journey from Millmead, the rafts pass under these double bridges at Ladymead on their way to the finish line at the Waterside Centre.

The previous bridge, which crossed the river at this point, embraced two arches and was demolished at the end of 1912.

The new bridge, with a single span, opened in September 1913. A small crowd of onlookers gathered on the towpath, possibly awaiting the arrival of Mayor George Odling Smee, who was to officially open the bridge. The child in the pushchair has a grandstand view at the front, and it seems the builders had not found the time to remove the central pier of the old bridge before the opening of the new one.

Up until about 1960 there was just one bridge across the Wey at Ladymead. This photograph, taken in 1957, shows work starting on the section of the dual carriageway from the railway bridge to the junction of Woodbridge Road, which led to the construction of a second bridge. To the right-hand side, behind the double-decker Aldershot and District bus, you can just make out the arch top of the bridge that spanned the original road to Aldershot. To the left of this picture is Woodbridge Meadows before the industrial development was built. Grays & Co car showrooms and workshop were built on this site next to the railway, and they traded there until around 2003. Travelodge opened a hotel here in 2005.

GUILDFORD CITY FOOTBALL CLUB

This 1960s aerial photograph gives a fascinating view of the area of Ladymead at that time. All the homes in the foreground have since given way to Europa Park, with superstores such as Homebase and B&Q. In the top right is Ingram Perkins Timber Merchants. It is now the home of Travis Perkins on part of the site and various other companies on the remaining land. Aldershot and District Traction Company bus garage is situated centre right. This became Alder Valley in later years, and Magnet Ltd trade counter and showroom currently occupy the site. In the top left is Guildford City Football Club ground in Joseph Road. A few years later in 1974, after this photograph was taken, the club folded. The wonderful pitch, which apparently was one of the best playing surfaces in south-east England, was dug up. The terraces and stand were demolished, and houses were built in their place in a road called Langley Close, named after the much-respected Guildford City player Jim Langley. The only other reminder that there was a football ground here is the City Social Club in Joseph Road.

Jim Langley played for City in the early 1950s and became one of the most successful post-war players. In 1952 he transferred to Leeds United for £2,000. He went on to play for Fulham in 1958, and he won three caps for England. Playing at full-back, he was one of a few footballers of the time who perfected the long throw-in, which would land in the goalmouth and often lead to panic in the opposing team's defence. This photograph shows a match between City and an All Star XI played at Joseph Road in April 1956. Langley turned out for the All Stars, and in this rare picture of him on the field of play, he is the player in the white shirt, in the centre, facing the ball.

This 1956 picture gives a good indication of how well Guildford City FC was supported over 50 years ago. The main stand appears to be full, and spectators on the terraces are shoulder to shoulder. Strangely enough, in the directors' box, shown to the left of the main stand, it always seemed to be standing room only. This was probably because there were not any seats there anyway. At least they were in a prominent position to receive any verbal abuse from the supporters, which happened quite often.

The team of 1963 won the Southern League Challenge Cup, which City also went on to win again in 1967. This was a great boost for supporters, who had not seen their team win the Southern League title since 1956. The only other time in their history that they accomplished this was way back in 1938. More success came with Cup football. Among their varied achievements, the London Football League Cup came to Joseph Road no less than four times between 1945 and 1950. Memorable FA Cup games against Football League opposition naturally drew the largest crowds. An FA Cup replay against Aldershot in the mid-1930s saw a record crowd of 9,932 pack into Joseph Road. City lost 4–3.

Three full-time players from the Cup-winning side of 1963 joined forces and formed a window cleaning business to supplement their wages. City manager Albert Tennant, who is kneeling down in the far right of the top photograph, sponsored them. Not only did the club have to find work for their players but also accommodation. Bad weather in January 1963 meant there were no football matches being played, and probably not any window cleaning either. David Cliss, former Chelsea golden boy, is cleaning the window, Peter Sillett, also from Chelsea and an international full-back, is holding the ladder and David Barrett, a useful inside-forward who gave great service to City, is the man with the bucket.

CORONA CAFÉ

Guildford City Football Club's demise in the 1970s was a great loss to many people in the town – it being a focus for social and community spirit. This brings to mind the much-lamented Corona Restaurant in High Street, which closed in 1978 to be replaced by a Pizzaland outlet. The Corona started life as a café towards the end of World War One. Within a few years it became the well-respected and popular Corona Restaurant.

The Corona of 1921 was a far cry from the restaurant that it was in the final few decades leading up to its closure. Its ground-floor atmosphere had probably remained the same for many years, though with men and women dining out and enjoying quality meals together. On the floors above, however, each room had its very own individual character.

Each floor was designated for different purposes. After ascending the antique staircase to the first-floor landing, you would find the bachelors' den to the rear of the building, complete with piano. This room was reserved for the 'young bloods' of Guildford. It was like a gentlemen's club smoking room, where important topics and pressing issues of the day were discussed.

The front room of the first floor had an altogether different clientele and atmosphere. Apparently, this room was a 'delightfully old-fashioned little room' and was reserved for ladies. Here, ladies would drink tea, away from the smoke and heavy discussions of the men's room opposite.

The wedding breakfast room on the top floor, fronting High Street, must have seen many a happy couple start their married life with a memorable celebration. It had elegant furnishings and an elevated view of the bustling High Street.

Anyone who remembers the Corona will appreciate this photograph of the top-floor room, with its original roof timbers dating back to at least the late 17th century. It was a pleasure to have a meal here, and you can imagine this room full of people sitting at the tables, relaxing and chatting with friends, having a great time and enjoying the surroundings. The February 1921 *Piccadilly Illustrated* stated that it was the 'quaintest of rooms, it boasts of conspicuous features which we do not suppose can be found in another café in the country'.

CORONA CAFÉ

**121 High Street,
GUILDFORD.**

THE "CORONA CAFÉ" is the favourite rendevous for residents, a fact which should recommend it to visitors. The Café is situated in one of the very oldest buildings in this locality, and in the large Dining Room may be seen Oak Beams dating from about A.D. 1520.

The Café has been furnished to match its "Old World Atmosphere," while the visitor will find the Catering fully equal to any in the West End of London, at Prices to please.

Parties up to 50 can easily be seated in one room.

COFFEE ROASTED DAILY.

AGENT FOR FULLERS.

PLEASE NOTE ADDRESS.

Corona publicity produced in the early 1920s boasted of its highest class of food preparation, with casserole cooking a daily feature. Owner Mr Ayers maintained the British public were unfamiliar with the virtues of a well-cooked omelette, but he found that ex-servicemen, who had returned after fighting in World War One, were very appreciative of them.

This is that same fabulous room in 2004 with those fine old beams hidden from view.

THORP'S BOOKSHOP

With the same degree of fond memories and great affection, Guildfordians remember Thomas Thorp's bookshop, which closed its doors for the last time on 25 January 2003. The bookseller's business had premises in High Street for nearly 100 years. For 17 years Thorp's had traded from a shop located on the corner of High Street and The Shambles, then in 1936 Thomas Thorp moved his business to this building facing High Street, which was the 19th-century Constitutional Hall. Here, the shop stayed for 67 years until it sadly ceased trading.

Unfortunately, in recent years not enough people came in to buy books. Large chain-store bookshops, with their ability to offer discounts, took the bulk of the market, and changing spare-time pursuits meant less people were reading books for pleasure. This photograph was taken two months before the shop closed, showing fewer books on offer and even fewer customers.

When you entered Thomas Thorp booksellers in its heyday, you were taken back in time. Thousands of books, old and new, were stacked from floor to ceiling. It was an Aladdin's cave of wonder! This 1980s photograph perfectly illustrates how every available space was utilised for the display of books on every subject imaginable. There was a real sense that the people who owned and worked in this bookshop were passionate about books. Customers came from far and wide to browse and buy new and second-hand books.

CONSTITUTION HALL

New Heights, a furniture store, took over the historic Constitutional Hall in 2006. The hall was originally built in 1886 for the Conservative Party to hold meetings in. In front of the hall a shop with a High Street frontage has been used by numerous businesses over many years, including outfitters and, between 1890 and 1901, the Surrey Drug Company's chemist shop, which dispensed potions from the premises. Interestingly enough, for a time in 1918 W.S. Mills used the building as a warehouse for the sale of new and second-hand furniture, and now it is again back to selling furniture but certainly not second hand. In the early 1900s the hall held concerts, public dinners and formal balls, although it is mainly remembered in that period as West's Picture Palace, Guildford's first cinema.

George Abbot's statue, which stands outside Constitutional Hall, was unveiled in April 1993 by Reverend Lord Runcie, Archbishop of Canterbury. He is probably the most well-known and respected Guildfordian whom the town remembers. Many books on Guildford have described the life of the man who built Abbot's Hospital across the road from where his statue now stands. He rose from humble beginnings to become Archbishop of Canterbury, but he never forgot his hometown and decided to found a hospital as a gift to Guildford, the place of his birth. When George Abbot died in 1633 at Croydon Palace, his will stated that he wanted to be buried in Guildford. When they returned his body to the town he loved, the townspeople granted his last wish, and he was interned in Holy Trinity Church.

HOLY TRINITY CHURCH

George Abbot's elaborate monument is situated at the east end of Holy Trinity Church; however, this is not where he is buried. The monument does not stand over the vault containing the archbishop's remains, as it had to be moved eastwards when a new chancel was erected in 1888. While work was in progress, workmen accidentally opened up the vault, and Archbishop Abbot's body was seen. Apparently his beard was still intact. Very few people were able to look into the vault and witness this remarkable sight as the brickwork was swiftly replaced. The vault, which had probably not been disturbed since his internment in 1633, was carefully resealed and is now underneath the front pews of the church.

Until the consecration of the cathedral on Stag Hill in 1961, Holy Trinity acted as the cathedral church for the Guildford diocese. With its prominent position in High Street, many ceremonious occasions are still performed on the steps outside.

Here, the church's steps act as a fitting backdrop to a regimental parade. On 4 June 1921 Guildford's local regiment, the Queen's Royal West Surreys, paraded before a memorial service in the church. The Queen's had had their barracks in Stoughton since 1881, training many local men before they went off to fight in World War One and Two, and then the Korean War between 1950 and 1953.

On 8 February 1952 Guildford marked Queen Elizabeth II's accession to the throne after her father, King George VI, had died. The High Sheriff of Surrey, Major F. Paget-Hett, read the proclamation at noon on the steps of Holy Trinity Church in front of a large crowd of local people. *God Save the Queen* was heard for the first time in over 50 years, and then the crowd gave a rousing three cheers for the new young queen.

WELCOMING THE VIKINGS HOME

In 1959, after 78 years of having their headquarters based at Stoughton, the Queen's Royal West Surreys withdrew from barracks and were absorbed into other regiments. The 1st Battalion The Royal Anglian Regiment, based in the borough at Pirbright, marched through Guildford on 27 November 2007 after their return from an arduous tour of duty in Afghanistan. Hundreds of people, young and old, stood in the pouring rain to give an emotional welcome home to the 1st Battalion, affectionately known as The Vikings.

Speeches were made next to the steps of Holy Trinity Church, including one by Major General Peter Everson, who said 'It was wonderful to see the people of Guildford celebrating the homecoming. The Battalion has enjoyed a close relationship with the town since 2001 and the presence of people at the parade is a testament to the strength of that relationship.'

The Bishop of Guildford, the Right Reverend Christopher Hill, gave the blessing. It was a poignant moment and a time to remember that during their six months tour of duty in Helmand Province nine soldiers from the regiment lost their lives, and a further 61 were wounded.

When the lines of troops set off from Holy Trinity Church to continue their parade, loud applause rang out from the crowd, showing their great respect and deep appreciation of The Vikings' service and commitment on the battlefields of Afghanistan.

Neither the regiment's band nor the hundreds of parading soldiers appeared to have any difficulty marching on High Street's uneven granite setts. Not even the wet conditions put them off their stride. In fact, quite the opposite, the troops welcomed the rain after six months spent in the intense heat of Afghanistan.

The troops marched off into North Street and continued on a circular route back to the parade's starting point at Town Bridge, where they stood down. At this point, many of the soldiers were reunited with their families. All 400 men were invited to a reception at the Guildhall with Mayor Mike Nevins and civic dignitaries, accompanied by their wives and girlfriends.

IN FRONT OF HOLY TRINITY CHURCH

Back in March 1930 there was a military presence of a different kind opposite Holy Trinity Church. Two soldiers on horseback marked the last Assizes being held in Guildford before their removal to Kingston. The trumpeters were preparing to play a fanfare at the end of the service being held in the church.

It is pleasing that we can still see morris dancing in the streets of Guildford, a tradition that dates back to the 15th century. On this occasion in 2004 the Pilgrim Morris Dancers are dancing outside Holy Trinity Church, entertaining the shoppers as they go about their business.

On this exact spot, in 1854, a very large bonfire was erected as part of Guildford's 'Guys' 5 November riots, which were a regular event in the 1850s and early 1860s. The Guys became more aggressive with their behaviour each year, and most locals stayed indoors on bonfire night with their curtains drawn and doors locked. The Guys were a gang of unruly young men who caused havoc, and the police could not control them. They would roam the streets in disguise, removing fences, gates and anything else flammable for

their fires. Large fireworks were made with dynamite and thrown at houses, sometimes with such force that they broke windows. Fights frequently broke out with other local youths, and it turned out to be a generally unpleasant night out in Guildford.

They excelled themselves with the 1854 bonfire by using wood removed from the old grandstand at Guildford Race Course on Merrow Downs. Eventually, after a policeman received serious injuries, soldiers were called to calm the rioters. With their help, police returned to the streets, armed with cutlasses. The ringleaders of the riots were caught and jailed. It turned out that many of the rioters came from well-respected local families. After 1865 the antisocial Guys were not seen on the streets again.

GUILDFORD RACE COURSE

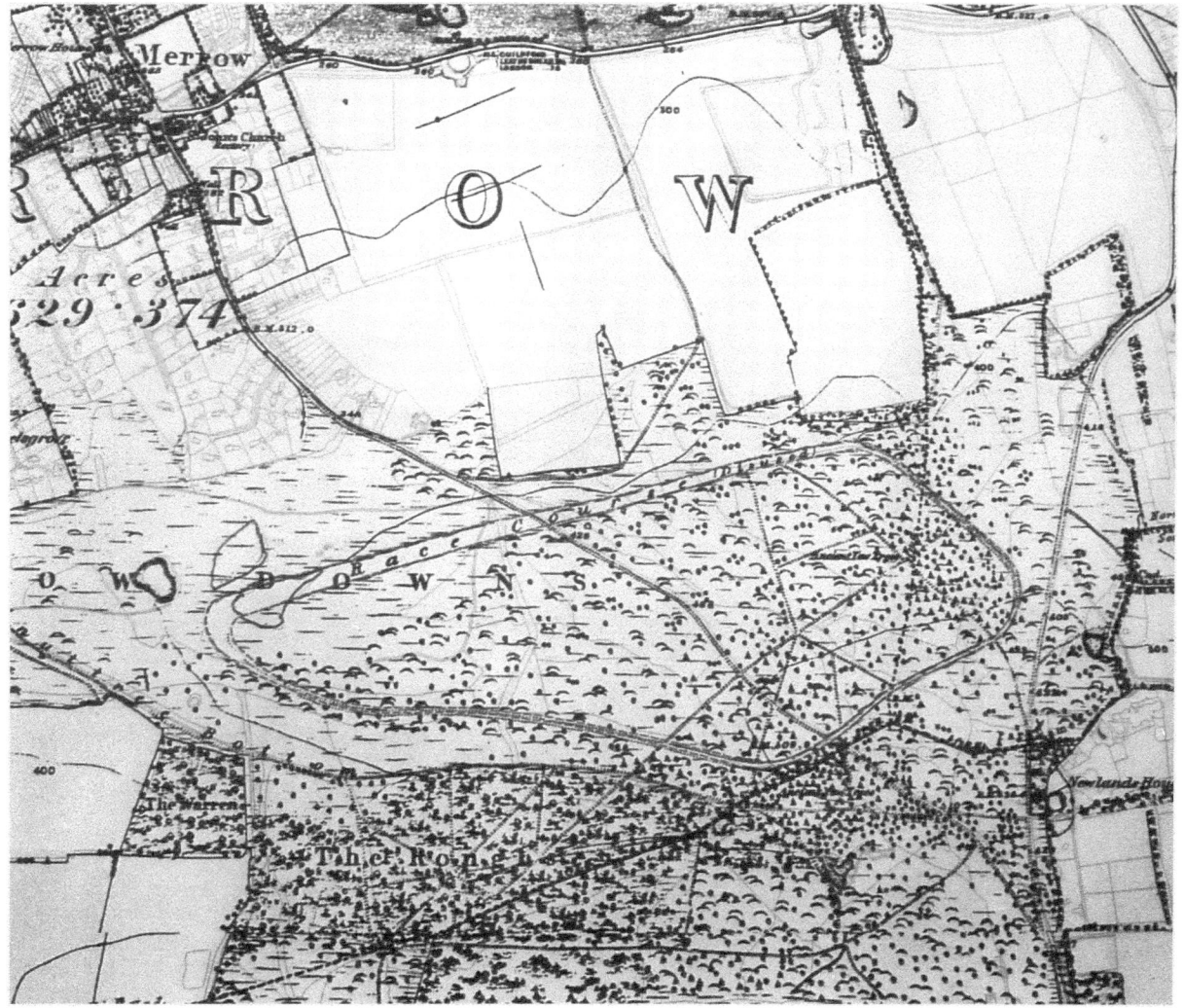

(The 2007 map of Merrow Downs is reproduced by permission of Ordnance Survey on behalf of HMSO. Crown Copyright 2008. All rights reserved. Ordnance Survey Licence number 100047957.)

The racecourse at Merrow ran over the Downs where Guildford Golf Club is now situated, crossing over Albury Road (Trodd's Lane) twice. The grandstand would have been positioned at the western end of the course's home straight, where the 10th fairway is today. Facing north, its views over Merrow and beyond would have been spectacular. Merrow's old chalk pit can be seen marked near to the course's sharp bend.

This wonderful Ordnance Survey map of a section of Merrow Downs is in fact a 2007 map superimposed onto one from 1870 showing Guildford Race Course. The first mention of horse racing on Merrow Downs was in an article in the *London Gazette* of February 1701. Whether this happened to be the first race meeting at Guildford's one-mile, seven-furlong track is just conjecture. In its heyday, Merrow's course attracted the finest racehorses of the 18th century, including the greatest of them all, Eclipse, whose name lives on with The Eclipse Stakes, which is held every July at Sandown Park. He had a short racing life, only entering 18 races, but he won them all. After retiring, he sired hundreds of race winners. Ninety-five per cent of today's thoroughbreds can be traced back to Eclipse – Desert Orchid and Arkle were just two of them. It had been said that Eclipse could run a mile in a minute and possessed a perfect temperament. In his time, he was described as 'the swiftest, most beautiful, the most perfect horse that the racing world had ever seen'.

Race meetings on Merrow Downs were formerly held at Whitsuntide, and large crowds of race-goers attended the event. These meetings also enjoyed royal patronage, and the winner of one of the main races was presented with The King's Plate, given originally by King William III, which included a 100 guinea purse. Eclipse won this race in 1770.

In 1718 King William rode on horseback from London, taking four hours to arrive at Clandon Park, where he stayed with Lord Onslow, so he could then attend the races on the Downs. He accepted Lord Onslow's hospitality for a few days, before returning to Kensington. Guildford Race Course started to decline in the late 1700s. In the 1800s Epsom and Ascot became more popular with the racing fraternity, and Guildford found it more and more difficult to finance the upkeep of the course. The last race on Merrow Downs was in 1870.

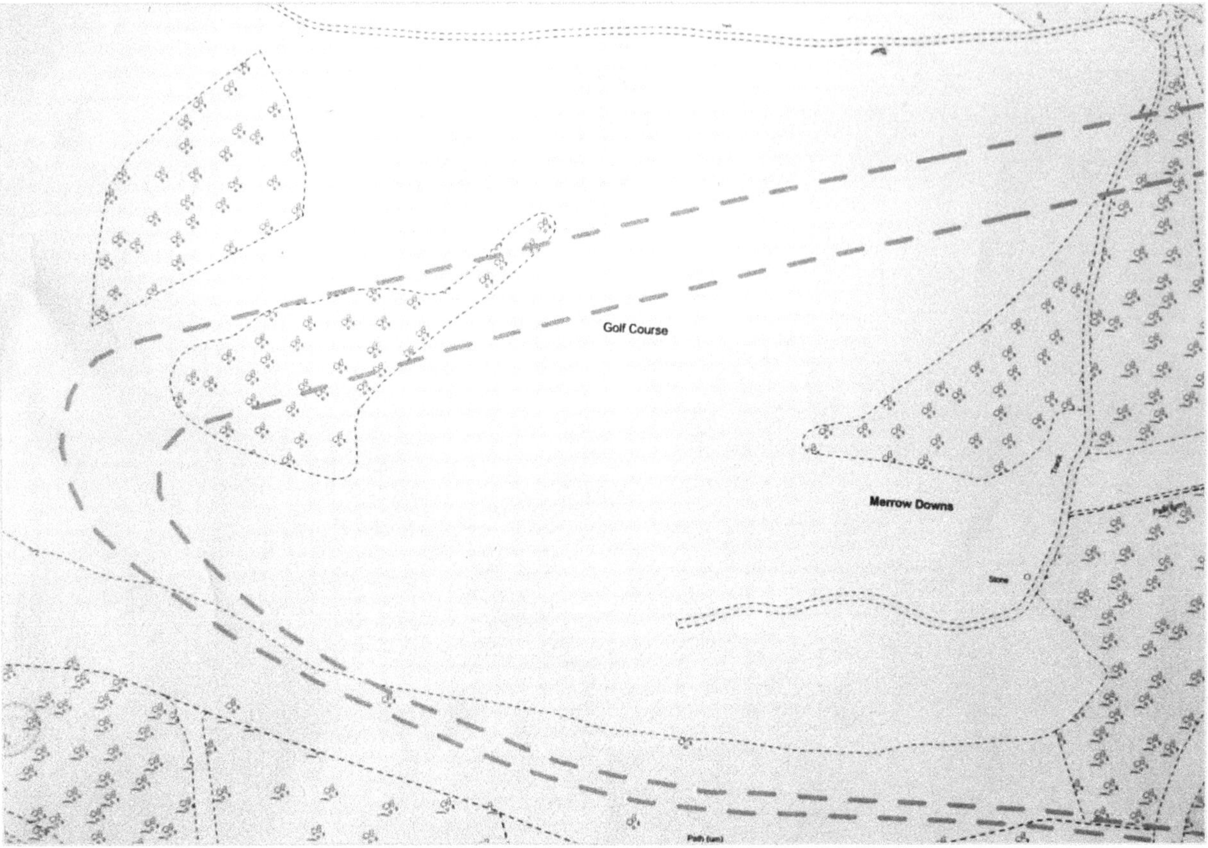

(This 2007 map of Merrow Downs is reproduced by permissions of Ordnance Survey on behalf of HMSO. Crown Copyright 2008. All rights reserved. Ordnance Survey Licence number 100047957.)

The horses would have sped across Trodd's Lane, top right, then uphill towards the winning post at the end of the straight on the left. For a second circuit they swung sharp left and then veered eastwards over the road again, shown lower right.

We know the exact location of Guildford Race Course on Merrow Downs, but where is the site of its elusive grandstand? The most likely position is the area seen on the left of this photograph, which is the approach to the 10th green on the golf course. It would have faced to the right with a fine view of the track's final furlongs, which ran through where the trees in front of the golfers are today. However, this is all conjecture on the author's part.

GUILDFORD GOLF CLUB

In 1886, 16 years after the last horse race on Merrow Downs, Guildford Golf Club was founded. Lord of the Manor, the 4th Earl of Onslow, gave his blessing to the venture, and at first there were just six holes laid out. Then six more were added fairly quickly, and by the end of 1888 the course had its 18 holes. Its first clubhouse, a house in Down Road, soon became too small for the increasing membership of the golf club, and a new clubhouse was built at the top of Warren Road in 1891. Just 10 years later, the clubhouse as it stands today, at the end of High Path Road, was opened to members. Here, ladies are practising their putting in front of the new clubhouse in 1902.

The original golf course covered ground from One Tree Hill eastwards towards Trodd's Lane but stopped some way short of crossing the road itself. Over the years the course has gradually moved away from the One Tree Hill area and continued further eastwards on the other side of Trodd's Lane, where holes six to nine were constructed in the 1930s. This photograph shows the eighth fairway down to the eighth green, with the ancient yew trees to the right-hand side. There are a few hundred yew trees on Merrow Downs, several of

which are said to be around 2,000 years old. In the 1930s Guildford golfers seemed to have a great sense of adventure. Two intrepid members set off on a two-hole match from Merrow to Bramley Golf Course and back in 1935, playing across fields and farms. They holed out on the 18th at Bramley, had lunch, then returned the same way back to hole out Guildford's 18th. On another occasion around this time, four members of the club, who had earlier attended a wedding, arrived at the club for lunch wearing morning dress. They then decided to play down High Path Road along Epsom Road and hole out in a water butt outside the Horse and Groom public house in their top hat and tails.

Merrow Village

These overdressed golfers probably popped into the Horse and Groom for a quick drink before returning to the Downs for a proper round of golf. One hundred years earlier, race goers would have travelled down from the racecourse, either to celebrate there with their winnings or maybe drown their sorrows in the pub. At that time the pub was called the Running Horse, or the Hare and Hounds before 1813. The building dates back to around 1650, and its outside appearance has changed very little over the centuries. By 1863 the pub went by the name of Horse and Groom. This photograph shows the pub and St John's Church at about the turn of the century, *c*.1900.

Travelling on the road back to Guildford, anyone returning from the races by carriage or on horseback may well have stopped at the village blacksmith for new horseshoes. Blacksmiths had occupied this site in Epsom Road since the 15th century. Mr Gould's forge was built in 1905, and the building survived until 1968. A petrol station now serves modern-day travellers from the same location. Forge Cottage, to the right, could have been Merrow's first public house.

ACCIDENTS ON THE EPSOM ROAD

Epsom Road became the scene of a tragic accident on 9 February 1911 when a steam traction engine careered out of control on the incline to the junction with Waterden Road. Mr William Collins of Epsom was transporting 12 tons of furniture packed on three trailers, which the engine was towing from Epsom to Southampton. Mr Collins stated that at the top of the hill his assistant warned him of a dip in the road near the Sandford Arms crossroads. The engine was then travelling at about 4mph, and the driver went to ease up by placing a pin in the gearing, which would put the engine into slow gear. Unfortunately, the pin slipped out, and the engine, as Mr Collins put it, 'got away' before he could fix in another pin. This happened at the Edgeborough Road junction, and by the time it had passed Austin Road the speed had reached 10 to 12mph. With the wagons swaying from side to side, the driver steered the engine into the kerb, and it mounted the footpath and crashed into a brick wall near Beech Lawn. It then swerved back on to the road and overturned. The driver and his mate, also men on the front of the second wagon, had miraculous escapes. Sadly, there was a wretched end to the incident. David Boxall from Epsom had been desperate in his search for work, and he had only just come out of Epsom Infirmary that morning, when he approached Mr Collins to ask him for a lift to Southampton to look for work. The driver readily agreed, and Mr Boxall sat on the tail board of the second wagon, but when the third wagon turned over in the crash he was caught by it and killed instantly.

Another accident on the Epsom Road occurred in 1927, but thankfully with less dire consequences. The 'Rural' bus on its way to Clandon, with 14 passengers aboard, collided with a car. Two women were slightly injured and were taken to the Royal Surrey County Hospital in Farnham Road.

ACCIDENT ON LONDON ROAD BRIDGE

A man had a very lucky escape from this crash in July 1928 on the London Road bridge over the railway line. This alarming incident, caused by a slippery road surface, and perhaps too much speed for the conditions, involved a fully-loaded 'Foden' steam wagon, complete with trailer. As it approached Guildford on its way to Peasmarsh, it skidded about 12 yards across the road and mounted the pavement. It smashed through the bridge wall and demolished 30 feet of brickwork, which landed on the railway lines below. The wagon came to a standstill, with the front wheel hanging precariously over the bridge's archway. The driver escaped without injury, but his mate apparently leapt from the cab and landed on the track 30 feet below in an effort to save himself from the impending crash. He was half buried under the falling debris but was rescued, unconscious, and rushed to hospital. Miraculously, he did not have any broken bones, but he did suffer a few internal injuries. Thankfully there were no trains due at the time of the crash, or the accident could have been much more serious.

It took two corporation steamrollers to haul the wagon clear of the bridge and then tow it away backwards to London Road station yard. It was estimated that over a ton of bricks were thrown on to the tracks below. Railway workmen from Guildford Station very quickly cleared the line, and there were only slight interruptions to the rail services. The bricklayers made a fine job of repairing the bridge wall and matching the existing bricks.

ACCIDENTS ON HIGH STREET

An accident on 11 December 1907 involved a lorry whose wheel lost grip on the High Street's granite setts, which resulted in its two trailers overturning and shedding their consignment of bricks on to the road in front of the Lion Hotel.

'Star Corner', at the junction of High Street and Quarry Street, became notoriously treacherous for heavy-duty vehicles with their solid wheels when trying to negotiate the downhill part of the High Street. Turning left into Quarry Street became quite hazardous at the best of times. When this lorry attempted the manoeuvre in February 1905, after a long period of rain, it seems it was positively dangerous.

LIFEBOAT DAY, 1904

The early part of the 20th century saw many heavy-duty, steam-driven vehicles, but horsepower still had its part to play in making the wheels turn. On 21 September 1904, which was Lifeboat Day, a lifeboat arrived at Guildford Station from Dover in preparation for a fund-raising event in the town. It is not known who supplied the horses to pull the boat, but they could well have been dray horses from the Friary Brewery or one of the other local breweries in the town.

A good crowd lined the High Street to witness the parade as it wound around the streets of the town. There were also a few steam engines in the procession, with Guildford and Woking fire brigades taking a leading part in the event with their fully-manned machines. Maybe, in today's world, we cannot imagine why the local population would dress up in all their finery and turn out to watch a procession around the town, but in the days before television this would have been an exciting and enjoyable day out for all townsfolk.

When the lifeboat arrived at Millmead, the horses were taken away for a well-earned rest. A band played to entertain the assembled crowds, while preparations were made to launch the boat into the river. There was great excitement as the lifeboat slipped into the Wey across from the Town Mill, and spontaneous cheering broke out as it touched the water. St Nicolas Church, seen on the right of the picture, gives a good indication of the launch site from the roadway.

After the lifeboat had turned in the Mill Pool, the crew brought it back alongside the roadway. Here a queue had already formed to take trips on the river for the cost of 6d (2½p) each. It appears that their excursion was very brief, travelling just downstream to the Town Bridge and back again. The trip might have been short, but the queue to have a ride in the Dover lifeboat was long. For about two hours, two boatmen rowed the vessel up and down the River Wey. In this picture, the lifeboat is heading downstream, passing John Moon's timber yard on its way to the bridge. The Debenhams store now stands alongside this stretch of river.

The cattle market at Woodbridge Road acted as a collection point for floats taking part in the afternoon's procession as well as an evening event. The route covered most of the town-centre streets and took about one hour to reach Millmead. An exciting incident occurred when a participant lit a cigarette and accidentally set fire to his magnificent moustache. The flame then set his wig alight, which he threw off, managing to set fire to two other men's wigs in the process! Luckily nobody was burnt.

Large crowds of people from neighbouring towns and villages arrived at Guildford Railway Station to watch the evening procession, which was similar to the afternoon's parade except for about 300 torchbearers who lit the way. There were a larger number of onlookers at the evening event, especially in the High Street.

HORSE DAY, 1910

It seems the citizens of Guildford in the early 1900s loved to celebrate, as we have seen, with parades and organised events for numerous reasons throughout the year. Horse Day on 25 May 1910, according to a *Surrey Advertiser* article at the time, 'was a bit of an eye opener to most people, that Guildford tradesmen could produce such a first class lot of horses. Most if not all looked in the pink of condition'. We must appreciate that horses at that time were a significant part of everyday life, and it would be in keeping recognising them with their own special day. The Horse Day parade had started from the cattle market in Woodbridge Road, proceeded along Friary Street, then climbed up High Street and wound its way back to the cattle market.

One might ask why there is a 2008 photograph of Onslow Street next to a 1910 picture of a Horse Day. Maybe now as the motor car has replaced the horse in our affections, it might seem fitting for society to celebrate with a Car Day each year? In fact both these photographs were taken from the same building in Onslow Street. At the present time, Harper's Nightclub occupies the property. From 1905 until around 1920 Shelvey & Co. Ltd, a mineral water business, traded from this building, and then up until the 1960s the *Surrey Times* had their printing works here.

CATTLE MARKETS

Woodbridge Road market acted as an assembly point for countless carnival processions and parades for over 70 years. It occupied the site opposite St Saviour's Church, and the town's sports ground was located here before the market opened in 1896. The sports ground moved to where we know it today, further along Woodbridge Road, in 1894.

Here are cattle waiting to be sold in 1896 on the last day of North Street's livestock market. They are tethered outside the rear access to the Castle Commercial Hotel, whose main High Street frontage is where Superdrug's store is currently situated. For about 40 years, from the 1930s until the 1970s, Jo Lyons tea room, one of the town's favourite meeting places, established itself in the same prime High Street position.

Here is another photograph showing North Street's cattle market on its last day in 1896 before moving to its new home on Woodbridge Road. It is interesting to see a gas lamp situated in the middle of the carriageway at North Street's junction with Woodbridge Road, but it was probably not a problem for the horse-drawn transport of the day. Animals were assembled in the area where later, in the first half of the 20th century, Colebrook & Co. butchers had their slaughterhouse.

Here are cars parked in the same spot in 2004, a far cry from the agricultural scene of the 1890s. Not too many of the buildings remain from the original photograph. Cloth Hall at the top of the street is one that has survived, but the Crown Inn, which had been attached to it and projected into the street, was removed in 1907. If you look carefully it is possible to see a few more buildings that remain. The Friary Centre extension will necessitate the demolition of all the buildings shown on the left side of the street.

BULLOCK IN HIGH STREET

Cattle from Woodbridge Road's market often had to be guided along Onslow Street towards the railway sidings at the station or up North Street to Colebrook's. In May 1909 a bullock ambled into Mr Paddison's High Street shop and walked the entire length of the shop floor. We must assume that he escaped from the drovers, either in Onslow Street or maybe from outside Colebrook's gateway, and not that he had just popped in for a new hat! A master butcher, who knew a thing or two about bullocks, was summoned to the shop. He relieved the tension by tickling the four-legged customer ever so gently under his tail. They say in the trade that this has a wonderful soothing effect on a bullock when he finds himself in a tight corner. After a few extra prods at his hindquarters, he left the shop after spending about 10 minutes inside. The adventurous bullock's fate is not known, but he left empty-hooved.

4 MAY 1909

Colebrook & Co., shown here in 1922, were not only butchers, but they also acted as poulterers, fishmongers and dealers in game. All these High Street buildings have survived into the 21st century, but none of the individual shops remain today.

SURREY ADVERTISER

To compile a book on a town's recent history, authors utilise the local newspaper's archives as an invaluable source of research information. The Guildford area is fortunate to have the *Surrey Advertiser* as its community newspaper. Their management and staff are very helpful to any budding historian with a genuine interest in Guildford's past. The newspaper transferred to Stoke Mill in 1999 from its town-centre location in Martyr Road.

This photograph, taken soon after the move, shows the top two floors and also the sympathetic restoration of this Grade II listed building. There is an opinion put forward that the box, fixed under the ridge at the top of the picture, is an original owl box that would have been installed by the old miller to encourage owls to roost and hopefully keep the mouse population down. Mills on the River Wey at Stoke have had a chequered history. This building, constructed in 1879, replaced a previous mill that burnt down in 1863. Just before Christmas 1931 part of the mill's south-east wall collapsed, complete with a few tons of wheat stored in a silo prior to milling. The collapse occurred in the afternoon, but fortunately none of the mill workers were injured.

In around 1870 the *Surrey Advertiser* opened its offices and printing works in Market Street after staying briefly at premises in Farnham Road and Sydenham Road. With an ever-expanding business, they moved to a new building in Martyr Road in 1937. In this 1980s photograph of Martyr Road the Art Deco style frontage can be seen on the left, and the old Biddles printworks is centre of the picture and was a very smart building in its prime. Unfortunately, it remained empty for years and ended up a total eyesore. Most people were relieved when it was eventually razed to the ground.

By 2001 these properties had succumbed to the demolition gangs, but work did not begin on a new development of a five-storey apartment block until 2005.

GUILDFORD INSTITUTE

An establishment that has been vital to the author and given him excellent access to local history documents is a treasure that Guildford could be in danger of losing. Guildford Institute has survived under many guises since 1834 when it was founded primarily to help educate craftsmen who lacked literary skills, through no fault of their own. It started life as Guildford Mechanic's Institute, but for most of its 174-year history it has been known as Guildford Institute. The institute's first home were rooms in the Angel Hotel on the High Street, but this accommodation did not prove ideal, and when Guildford's first public hall opened in North Street they eagerly transferred there in around 1845. In the 1890s the Guildford and Working Men's Institute (its name at the time) purchased the Temperance Hotel on

the corner of North Street and Ward Street for the sum of £2,250 from the Reverend Francis Paynter, who we met earlier during our Beating the Bounds expedition. The photograph above was taken in 1881 and shows the Royal Arms Temperance Hotel's official opening on 20 July by the Earl of Onslow.

The institute soon set to work on arranging finance to extend the building along Ward Street. Guildford Technical Education Committee offered £500 but the costs escalated, and apparently the town withdrew from the agreement, which left the institute owing quite a large sum of money. The president of the institute, the Duke of Northumberland, kindly lent funds to clear the debt, and the institute was then able to repay the money over a period of years. It was not until 1917 that the final instalment of the loan was paid.

The institute's reading room in the 1920s provided up to 25 daily newspapers, various journals and periodicals for members. From the early 1800s it served as Guildford's main library, because the town did not possess its own public library. To have access to the extensive collection of books, it was necessary to pay your 'subs' and join the Guildford Institute. Apparently there were times when non-members used the facilities, which caused quite a stir among some paying members. Eventually, day tickets were issued to non-members, which allowed them to use the library for a small fee, and this seemed to have satisfied all concerned.

The room is now referred to as Assembly Room, where a variety of events and activities are held, including talks, recitals, exhibitions and so on. On Monday to Friday lunchtimes during term-time the room transforms into a vegetarian restaurant, with a selection of tasty homemade dishes. University of Surrey's financial support since 1982 had insured that Guildford Institute continued to have an important role to play in the life of Guildford; however, another setback befell the institute in 2008 when the university revealed that they could no longer help with future financing and withdrew their funding. It is important to mention that it is doubtful whether the institute would have survived into the 21st century if the university had not stepped in with their help in 1982.

Ever since the early days, the institute has had a chequered history. In the 1800s there were divisions that threatened its continuing existence and then amalgamations that strengthened the establishment. Until World War Two, the institute remained a cultural centre for the town, becoming a meeting place for local societies and public lectures, and the building even contained a small museum. Then gradually the functions of the institute declined, and its membership dwindled. In the 1970s there was another revival, with added enthusiasm from members to create a more vibrant institute, and with interest in local history growing, the future looked bright. But then disaster struck in 1989 with the discovery of dry rot in the building. This is when the University of Surrey came to the institute's aid.

Clare Mills, the institute's librarian from 1998 to 2006, seen here at her desk, worked particularly hard to help modernise the running of the library and at the same time look towards the conservation of the institute's impressive collection of old books. During her active period as librarian, Clare ensured that the local history collection became much more accessible for researchers to locate material. With the recent surge in interest in genealogy, the library is an invaluable source of information for people tracing their family history and finding out what life was like for their ancestors. The institute's library has always been the jewel in its crown, ever since its humble beginnings.

In 1903 membership soared to a grand total of 1,576, and the library held over 10,000 books. At the present time there are just 500 members but over 13,000 books on the shelves or in safe storage, waiting to be discovered and explored. A few years back, the institute had to sell a number of its old volumes to help pay for the maintenance of the property. Guildford Institute is a special institution, something that should be cherished by its town, as it is such a great asset. It has had many highs and lows since 1834, and without a doubt it must continue to serve the people of Guildford for many future generations to come.

Without Guildford Institute's marvellous local history collections, *Guildford Life Past and Present* would never have materialised.

BIBLIOGRAPHY

Alexander, Matthew *Guildford As It Was*, Hendon Publishing Co. Ltd, 1978.

———— *More Surrey Tales*, Countryside Books, 1986.

Burkitt, Reverend Henry J. *The Story of Stoughton*, 1910.

Chamberlain, Russell *Survival. The Rise, Fall and Rise of the Guildford Institute of the University of Surrey*, Piton Publishing House Ltd, Godalming.

Collingwood, Jeremy *Francis Paynter – A Remarkable Guildfordian.*

Guildford Golf Club booklet, 1986.

Guildford Institute Archives.

Hutchinson, Philip *Haunted Guildford*, Tempus Publishing Ltd, 2006.

Merrow Residents Association *Merrow Downs*, 1991.

Oakley, W.H. *Guildford In The Great War*, Billings and Sons Ltd, Guildford, 1934.

Observer Sport Monthly, March 2007.

Rose, David *Guildford Our Town*, Breedon Books, 2001.

Sturley, Mark *The Breweries and Public Houses of Guildford*, Charles W. Traylen, Guildford, 1990.

Surrey Advertiser Archives.

Taylor, Brian *The Lower Church*, 1986.

BV - #0126 - 280426 - C0 - 276/195/12 - PB - 9781780913612 - Gloss Lamination